Wisdom Has a Voice:

Every Daughter's Memories of Mother

Wisdom Has a Voice:

Every Daughter's Memories of Mother

Edited by Kate Farrell

Introductions by

Amber Lea Starfire & Caryn Mirriam-Goldberg

First Edition Paperback
ISBN-13:
978-1-58832-217-3

This fine book and many others are available at:
www.unlimitedpublishing.com

To my brother, John Fischer (1946-2010), a mountain climber and guide, who one day urged me up a steep granite cliff, beyond my safe boundaries and past my fears.

Contents

Introduction

Kate Farrell

M *other* is the silent icon of our times. Shrouded in myth or dehumanized by high expectations, she often remains hidden from view. Daughters whisper about *Mother* to friends, vent about her to therapists, or honor her with reverence and respect. But in all cases, mothers matter to their daughters and it is through their eyes that we can begin to see the mothers around us. We discover who she really is and learn from *Mother*.

This compelling collection of twenty-five memoirs about mothers written by their daughters reveals a legacy between them. The stories run the gamut of mother-daughter relationships, from the most tenderhearted to abusive, from deep rapport to discord. Yet each story tells an authentic truth, extracts an understanding, finds wisdom.

Divided into two sections, *Mother Love* and *Mother Loss*, this anthology contains a worldwide variety of voices from lighthearted to poignant. Through daughters' honest stories, the myths about *Mother* dissolve and we see that mothers are, in fact, real people. Though we may demand of *Mother* that she love us perfectly, the amazing and more interesting revelation is her imperfect humanity. We may expect *Mother* to be flawless, to not have a shady past, a dark side, or even a separate life, but in these stories we find mothers who are simply people with needs, their own history, and palpable vulnerabilities. Knowing mothers as multidimensional women in many ways makes them even more significant.

There are common threads of wisdom in this tapestry of international tales. We discover them in the context of extraordinary memoirs written with care and skill, each writer bringing insight into her experiences with mother or a mother figure. Enjoy these true tales—they are women's stories about mother we've been waiting for.

SECTION ONE
Mother Love

Introduction: *Mother Love*

Amber Lea Starfire

A mother understands what a child does not say.

— Jewish proverb

I remember standing in front of a rack of Mother's Day cards opening card after card, but failing to find a card that would adequately express my feelings about my mother. None held the right words. So, I went home and wrote words of my own, a child-ish poem of apology and appreciation. My mother framed that poem and hung it on her wall—not because my words had poetic merit of their own, but because her love for me elevated them to display-worthy status.

What *is* a mother's love? A mysterious and enduring force, it springs from the fathomless depths of a woman's being. It gives her the ability to divine her children's hopes and fears when the children are not able to do so for themselves. It compels her to put herself last in order to nurture her children, keep them safe and healthy, and guide them to achieve their dreams. It requires her to use skills that, if she's lucky, she learned from her own mother.

In the following pages, a mother's love is defined in the com-ingled voices of thirteen diverse women—many who became mothers themselves and passed this legacy of love to their own children. These women writers reflect on the wisdom, strength, and life lessons they received from their mothers.

Common themes thread their way through all these essays. It's not the words mothers say, but their actions that mean the most. It's in small ways—hugs and kisses, a favorite piano melody, a warm smile at the right time—that they model their values, ease life's painful moments, soften hearts, and encourage their young charges. Through these writers' stories and viewpoints, readers are empowered to see their own mothers with renewed vision as heroes who guide with compassion and who show through example how to be tender, caring human beings. Heroes who are willing to help others in need, and—even—to break down the social barriers of elitism and prejudice.

> . . . every person in our neighborhood, in our world, was treated as a person worthy of respect. From Mom, I learned . . . that we must respect each other's feelings, appreciate our likenesses and differences, and that we must treat others as we want to be treated ourselves.
>
> — Shelley Chase Muniz, "Even Then"

> I think that my mother quietly invented random acts of kindness.
> — Pat Jackson-Colando, "A Kiss and a Hug"

> Over the years, I've observed how she treated each person who came into her life. Her example of love and care for others was her most endearing gift to me, second only to the very life she gave me.
> ~Barbara Kitscher, "Endearing Gift"

> None of the . . . girls had ever been in a private home with Negroes and whites together. . . . We had broken old barriers.
>
> — Jeanne Jusaitis, "Liebestraum"

Patience is a common trait of loving mothers. For Rebecca Milford, redemption from anorexia came to her through her mother's patience and unwillingness to pass judgment on her daughter. Instead, her mother quietly showed her daughter a different way.

> I am learning to understand myself, and what it means to have a problem. . . . I am getting better, and she is the reason for this.
> — Rebecca Milford, "Quiet Morsels with My Mum"

Many loving mothers display undiminished optimism and fortitude in the midst of life's troubles. These qualities are particularly significant for writers whose mothers died far too young or lived through long illnesses—mothers who bore their illnesses bravely, cheerfully making time for their children. Memories of these mothers' unconditional love, warm smiles, and daily routines have buoyed our writers throughout their lives, and they have carried precious, inherited lessons into their own motherhoods.

> Unconditional love is the best gift I could have received from her. . . . Knowing that I parent like my mother makes me feel closer to her.
>
> — Danielle Christopher, "Motherless Moments"

> . . . your spirit remained indomitable. Until the very end you maintained that everything would be all right, that soon your problems would be over.
>
> — Mariana Swann, "Finding You Again in Bolivia, October 2010"

> "Be present for those you love. Never give up hope. Value the time you're given."
>
> — Diane Hurles, "The Bed"

Daughters want to please their mothers and make them happy, but sometimes mothers seem too demanding and difficult to please. That is, until we watch them remain strong for others, even as they deal with the deaths of their own mothers. Such was the revelation for Angela Tung, in her story "Puo-puo." We've all heard about the child on the bus who asks her mother in an embarrassingly loud voice why that woman is so fat, or why that man carries a white cane. Sara Etgen-Baker, in "Journey with Mother," tells us what it's like to have a mother who listens to her questions and uses these potentially embarrassing moments to patiently instruct her daughter. Hers was a mother who answered difficult questions with tact and care about society's ugly side. A mother who embraced and modeled courage for her child.

There is another kind of courage, as well: Suni Paz learned from her mother to trust her heart and follow its guidance. This precious advice enabled Suni to be a substitute mother for her students. She was able to help one child in particular, who was far away from his mother, to achieve his dreams. And she was able to show all her students to be.

> . . . loving, compassionate, helping, and reassuring . . . above all to open their hearts and listen to one another. These were the values I learned from my mother . . . . Now I was passing them on to my students.
>
> ~Suni Paz, "Let the Heart Speak"

As one of seven children, Barbara Kitscher always felt cherished. Her mother had been told that she would never give birth. As a result, she saw each child as a miracle, each child as someone to be loved and treated with respect. For many women like Barbara, there is a connection between a loving mother and her sense of spirituality or love of art.

> . . . the qualities she wanted for herself: to be a good mother, to be dependable, grounded, nourishing and trustworthy, and to be spiritual.
>
> ~Suni Paz, "Let the Heart Speak"

> All of us were seen and watched over as precious gifts from God.
>
> ~Barbara Kitscher, "Endearing Gift"

> God and faith sustained her through many hard years . . . . This, she says, is the most important part of your life: your faith in God.
>
> ~Maria Klassen, "What More Could a Daughter Ask?"

> I would come to value my mother's love and dedication to her music that inspired me to succeed in bringing my childhood dance fantasies to fruition. I would eventually teach classical ballet, modern dance, and choreography . . . affirming for students the power of the arts to positively influence their lives.
>
> ~Linda Sievers, "Life Is What You Make It Be"

Another common thread is appreciation for mothers who helped their daughters learn limits through firm discipline and natural consequences for negative behaviors.

It seemed I found myself sitting in the corner whenever my mother got upset because I had disobeyed . . . .

~Linda Sievers, "Life Is What You Make It Be"

My mother's warnings about safe boundaries were clear as I tested the waters of freedom.

~Shelley Chase Muniz, "Even Then"

Love lessons are worth more than a million oceans.

~Danielle Christopher, "Motherless Moments"

Taken together, these daughters' stories paint a portrait of Mother at her best—the mother whom everyone hopes to have—understanding, supportive, involved, adventurous, and brave enough to overcome her own troubles. Not perfect, not a saint, but habitually patient and kind and able to view life through her children's eyes. Read on, to view this rich and vividly colored portrait of Mother Love.

A Kiss and a Hug

Pat Jackson-Colando

*A*ll it takes is a little kiss. Not an amorous smacker with movie star alignment or one of great slobber quality from your favorite dog. Just a little one, preferably harmonized with a hug.

That's what my mother taught me. Implicit in her way and better than the doctrine of an apple a day, I think that my mother quietly invented random acts of kindness. She kept it in-house as her family formed and grew, and then reached into the world beyond her "chickens" when we flew.

"Come here," she'd say with a smile, arms open wide and ready. "Tell me about your day," and I did. Cares went away, faults and facts were mediated, feelings were soothed, tempers quelled. It was better than milk and cookies.

Mother had four children, correction—she had five, because my father was a child in many ways. He was brilliant, narcissistic, and openly manic-depressive. His loud, red-faced yelling was scary to a child. He'd been a small man through the ridicule of high school years, having to settle for being a cheerleader in high school while his taller classmates battled on the basketball court, the sport of kings in Indiana. He yearned always to accomplish feats large in life. He had the stigma of his stern, self-absorbed father to surmount and a legacy of family farming to escape.

My father's father was generous in his gift of a farm when my parents married after the war. But my father knew that he was generous with criticism and complaint as well. Though the horse-whip would have likely been sheathed in respect for a son who'd fought for his country, Grandpa's words were terse—and things always seemed to go from bad to worse between father and beholden son. Especially in a small town with Grandpa's name and everyone a relative with opinions to speak. Thanks but no thanks, my parents said, we've heard of the GI Bill and its educational promise.

So they traded barns and buildings among open, flat fields for hastily built married student housing that was a hundred miles away. Camaraderie with collegiate veterans rather than communion with cows at 4:00 a.m. or sowing fields with corn, alone on a tractor for what seemed like days. Straining to learn new subjects rather than straining to grow crops

Pat's mother, Katherine Louise Moeller Jackson

amidst Mother Nature's weather changes in the southern hill country. Courses over coarseness: the education felt erudite, just right to rebuild the American dream lost in the wounds of war.

My maternal grandparents were educators and that's the field my father pursued after he and Mother married, trading one flawed family heritage for another, perhaps. The vocation had its rewards and its struggles. My mother was perpetually supportive, ardently, patiently, earnestly juggling everything with calm and aplomb. "How was your day, dear?" with a smile, a kiss, and a hug. It was better than a beer.

Mother had a Depression-era working mom who played bridge and tended her plants better than her two children. My grandmother was a high school home economics teacher, but she never sewed or cooked family meals with any great talent. My mother preferred the title of Mother, as did my grandmother, with all of the German formality that it implied. But never mind the houseplants. She learned to cook like my father's doting mother and to sew my clothing, the better to sustain our family on one salary. "Yes, dear, I will. I must. I can," with a smile, making do in the way of the fifties.

Her father was reportedly stern and foreboding, although I observed my grandpa more as an artisan crafter of soaps and caned chairs, his avocations in retirement. He awarded dimes for A's on report cards, treasures that were easy for me to collect. At report card time, "Please, can we go to Grandpa's?" I'd ask, often with a smile and a kiss to sweeten the request, following my mother's model.

Grandpa welcomed us to his home, with the open, refurbished attic so like a cavernous college dorm room with sleeping bunks and beds. When his two daughters married, they'd moved some distance, so the remodel was canny inducement to come and stay awhile. Grandpa was always faintly smiling, as if he were humming along with the merry rhythms of children playing, laughing, and reading books. The dorm was lined with bookshelves heavy with hidden worlds. "May I take this one home, Grandpa? I didn't get to finish it in the hours we were here."

But, of course, Mother and I finished our books in a few days after we'd gotten home and craved more to read. She queried my teacher and her friends, concocting a solution for our problem.

"Let's get the children library cards in Geneva," Mother suggested to Father with a smile.

"That's too far to drive every week," he grumped. "And the little one is only three."

"But we have to get groceries anyway and everyone says that the IGA has the best prices, so we could save despite the thirty miles to drive. Perhaps we could leave the children at the library during story hour while we get the groceries." Then, she crossed the room to give him a hug and a little kiss.

We went to the library weekly. The vistas within books extended the borders of our tiny town and we all grew accustomed to the magic. Reading helped to while away hours of winter chill and spring rain, but then summer came and it was time to be out-of-doors.

"I need a way to get milk and a loaf of bread sometimes," said my mother who didn't drive. "I was thinking that Patty could run the errand for me if she had a bike," Mother ventured in the summer I was seven. My father's face broadened into a smile to match the one my mother wore when she delivered her hug and little kiss. What a good idea he'd had!

I can still see my father's pride as he walked a big blue bike up the sidewalk to our back porch. I can feel the shared joy as he helped me learn to ride on the paved semicircle drive and huge expanse of lawn. His arms around mine on the handlebars, sending me off on the journey. This felt like a hug and I saw him smiling broadly as I learned to pedal unaided. I could ride to the grocery, the park, or my friends' homes; I could go on my own in my small, small world. It was freedom and it was responsibility, all in my shiny blue bike.

"The Millers got a cocker spaniel and their children really have fun with him," I heard soon thereafter.

"We barely have enough money to feed ourselves, let alone an animal." My father described himself as a no-nonsense man. What was true was that he always began with "no."

"Marie says that Buster eats their table scraps and loves to gnaw on the roast beef bone," Mother continued.

"But I grew up having to care for all of those animals on the farm. And we kids were sure that my dad loved his hunting dogs more than he loved us. I don't want to be around that again!"

"I've seen your father and how he dotes on those dogs. But your mother always seems to get new clothes and such. I'll bet you did, too," she said as she reached in for a hug. A big smile followed by a little kiss. My mother had the sense to go beyond his "no."

Our dog's name was Buffy. He often went along with me when I rode to the small grocery three blocks from our house, then back again with a sack of groceries in the handlebar basket. Our hair was almost the same color. We must have made quite a pair, making our own jet stream through the streets of the town. I never tired of the riding, though it was within a mile square. Buffy enjoyed the run, but he waddled some, due to the table scrap feed. Dogs are constant good sports and he was my golden shadow.

Woven into the chat during the supper meal one evening: "I heard that the Mennonites are having six weeks of Bible School in

July. This would be good for Patty. They have the children memorize passages of scripture, so she'll keep up her skills." Mother gave my father his little kiss and hug, but I don't think that he was even mouthing a protest; such was the value of strong academics in our family.

"Patty will need a new dress because she was chosen to recite a Bible verse on the final program night."

"Why can't she wear the blue one she got for Easter?"

"Because she's grown two inches this summer, dear. Buffy has grown fatter, but Patty hasn't. She's grown up. It's a wonder since they both run a lot," Mother mused, then gave my Dad a little kiss to accompany her puzzled smile.

She got a new dress, too, the better to be the proud mother of the daughter in the new dress in the front row on the stage. No matter that the daughter had cut off her bangs in an unthinking moment of being seven and hasty. During the rest of the summer, as Buffy shed his heavy winter coat, I was accused and re-accused of cutting my hair. Oh well, it grew back, as did my sister's.

Wash the new dresses and the other weekly laundry and hang them out on the clothesline by the white picket fence—dry cleaning wasn't considered. "The best tan I ever got was when I had to wash diapers daily," Mother said with a smile in later years. The negative always became a positive, earlier or later. And a little kiss for my father as he came in from mowing the lawn—never coincident with the laundry day—along with the lemonade that he relished. A peck of reassurance for a man who was never filled with self-confidence, no matter what his façade.

"Did the barn painting go well?" Mother asked in Father's ear as she hugged him, speckled clothes and all. She kissed his lips, the only place that seemed to be untouched by paint. My father was admittedly a "slap-dash" man, unused to the precision of painting. But it was a good summer income for a teacher, what my mother's father had done.

"I saw an article in *Life* magazine about Mammoth Cave in Kentucky. Did you realize that it's been a national park for fifteen years? It would be a good day trip after we visit your folks and mine to celebrate Grandparents Day. I know it's a Hallmark invention, but it's a good excuse to visit them. We haven't been in a while. The baby is due in another month, so we won't be able to travel to see our folks for a while after that," Mother said.

"I don't want to put the miles on the car." The car was a two-tone green 1957 Chevrolet that was new to our garage.

"But Dinah Shore said to see the USA in your Chevrolet." Dinah Shore was one of my Dad's favorites because he'd met her while on leave during the late days of the war. Mother expanded her arm, "throwing" a kiss the length of the supper table, in imitation of Dinah's famous television gesture. My father grinned back.

We all got new sunglasses before the trip and we must have packed some suitcases, for the trip to Mammoth Cave extended to a week that included a visit with some friends who lived near Louisville. I can visualize the expanses of the white fence trademark of horse farms as we drove the countryside. I doubt if we attended the Derby. I still have the Mammoth Cave slide collection and my childhood View Master to refresh my memory of that road trip, the first of many with my vagabond dad.

There were the weekly Sunday afternoon road trips, a wind through country farm roads set at right angles around our small town. My father had a secret smile as we drove and drove and drove. I was perpetually lost and mystified that we always got back to the "right place"—our home—in about an hour.

What a wonderful way to give my mother a respite on Sunday, the Lord's Day of rest. What a wonderful way to be in action, but not to relate with feeling for your children, in the stolid way of the fifties. Refreshed, my mother would greet us all with open arms and a little kiss when we were just barely inside the back porch door.

"I heard there's a new restaurant over near Geneva. Perhaps we could take the children there for our anniversary." Hug and smile and kiss.

The restaurant's sign shines bright in my memory. It was a windmill of blue neon and looked just like the logo on my favorite brand of cookies. I wore my special Bible School dress and tried to use the silverware in proper sequence. It was a meal that began in prayer and ended in a hug and a smile and a kiss for everyone. The anniversary dinner shared with their children became my parents' rite, almost as worship for their union.

Mother gave little kisses with hugs as part of her regular household chores, creating harmony in our lives. I realize now, as I remain enthralled in the special relationship that I share with my husband (the envy of all our friends), that my siblings and I chose mates wisely because my mother modeled how to be friendly and firm, direct and gentle, and to seal it with a kiss. Good times, bad times, always a positive undercurrent. Her good nature and good nurture made simple the way to bliss—you seal it with a kiss, just a little kiss.

Even Then

Shelley Chase Muniz

Three perfect little girls, ages ten, eight, and six, dressed in blue jeans, t-shirts, and sneakers, hair curled but mussed and spoiled with bits of dry leaves. We ran, hearts pounding, chased by a henna-haired lunatic with a broom in her hand, screeching, "I'll get you, you little mongrels!" My feet leapt over uncharted territory as my mind gripped the reality of our criminal mischief. "Vandals! Get back here!" roared Mrs. Hawkins. "Wait until I tell your mother!"

It was 1960. School was out for the day. My mother had cooked chocolate pudding as an after-school snack. When my two sisters and I arrived home, she took a break from work, got our snack, and made sure that we started our homework before we began to play. We were fortunate in that we lived next door to our family business. A simple trip out the back door of the house, down a short path to the back door of our grocery store, and Mom and Dad were right there, available whenever we needed them. Mom was a working mother, but as the store was an extension of our home life, we hardly noticed.

Our corner grocery store was one of the originals in Modesto, California, with the old-time traditions of taking orders over the phone and hand-delivering groceries. Every morning my mother made phone calls to our elderly customers, checking on their health and inquiring about their grocery needs. Around noon she would arrive on their doorsteps and if no one answered her knock, she would enter the house, unload the groceries, and place perishables in the refrigerator before leaving. An itemized list written on a duplicate receipt was left on the kitchen table. It was Mom's simple yet efficient way of bookkeeping and notifying customers of what they owed.

My father opened the store at 8 a.m. Monday through Saturday. He quickly busied himself by turning on lights, adding change to the cash register, opening the lids on the freezer boxes, choosing and purchasing produce off the trucks of local farmers. Meanwhile, my mother took care of her daughters. She made us breakfast, ironed our dresses, packed our lunches, gave us kisses and hugs, and watched as we made our way up the sidewalk toward the neighborhood elementary school. We waved good-bye to her multiple times, checking to make sure she was still standing in front of the house—verifying her presence all the way to the end of the sidewalk, the irrigation canal that marked the perimeter of our safety zone.

Shelley and her mother, Nellie Zukal, April 2011

This irrigation canal was our signal to take things seriously and pay attention to our surroundings. You could drown in that canal. And beyond the canal were houses where strangers lived and roads where cars drove too fast. Our neighborhood was sublime, lined by huge sycamore trees that arched from one side of the street to the other with paradelike grandeur. The houses were bungalow style with porches for shade and fenced yards in which the children played. But the canal marked a change my mother emphasized with persistence. Beyond the canal was the world outside.

I was aware that, as I left for school, my mother's life shifted. That's when she became a working mom. Without complaint, she managed her day and her family's needs: the grocery store, sewing, cleaning, and cooking, without ever a complaint. She never became surly, even as my sisters and I grew into moody teenagers.

At the store, Dad tended the fruits and vegetables, removing the outer leaves off heads of lettuce; arranging tomatoes, cucumbers, onions, potatoes; stacking apples, strawberries, cantaloupes, and nectarines. Mom manned the checkout counter, made her phone calls, put orders in brown shopping bags, and got them ready to deliver. As Dad worked at his butcher block, creating displays of pork chops, trussing chickens, cutting beef roasts and steaks, and laying out trays of hot dogs and baloney, Mom swept the front entryway, rang up sales as customers finished perusing her carefully organized shelves of canned goods, and kept the books when she had spare time.

Families had charge tags and children called our store the "free store," without ever realizing that the groceries they picked up for their parents were actually paid for. The Quality Food Store, nicknamed *The Little Green Store* by locals, was a landmark, a place neighbors used as a starting point when they gave driving directions to their friends. People used the store as a meeting place; parents told their kids to come and see "Nell and Chuck" if they ever needed help, that Nell and Chuck would know what to do and who to call in case of an emergency. My parents were at the center of The Little Green Store's reputation: my father, wearing his bow ties and white butcher's apron; my mother, with her gray curls swept into an up-do, her simple dresses and soft leather walking shoes.

As the nickname suggested, the store was painted a happy green. It was always clean and orderly, inside and out. Stocking the shelves was a job relegated to my sisters and me. Once homework was done and playtime was over, we would go to work in the store, checking shelves for empty holes, restocking them from a supply we kept in a back storage room: cans of Campbell Soup, Del Monte Creamed Corn, Green Giant Peas. Little boxes of Jell-o Tapioca, Star-Kist Tuna, and Hormel Deviled Ham. Mom would work beside us, teaching by example. Her warm smile, honesty, and thoughtful consideration of her customers' needs were woven into a fabric of pride and professionalism. Together we would rotate the cans and boxes on the shelves, placing the old in front of the new, dusting and cleaning. I loved the store's small assortment of lipsticks and mascara, imagining what brand I might use when I grew up, what shade of blush I might rub on my face.

My sisters and I learned to use the cash register, to count out money and give change, to put the customer's needs first. Always. We learned a strong work ethic during those years; we knew our place within our family business and accepted it as both an honor and a necessity. Most importantly, my mother's philosophy of kind acceptance seeped into our lives by daily examples. Her thoughtfulness was something that happened without an effort. Every person in our neighborhood, in our world, was treated as a person worthy of respect. Mom accepted everyone for who and what they were: an extension of family. I saw this in her actions, heard it in the tone of her voice, in the words she spoke. "We are all just people," she would say. "No one person is better than the next simply because of his or her station in life or the color of his or her skin."

Old Ben, the homeless alcoholic who came daily to our store hoping for a handout, was never disappointed. Mom had a sandwich ready for him and a cup of coffee to comfort his jittery nerves. She never asked Ben for money, but often he would take her broom and sweep the sloped entry to the store as payment. On days he was too shaky to manage, he would sit and eat and drink, resting his sore back against the wood siding on the front of the store.

"Why do you let that bum sit out there like that?" asked Joan Finkle one day. "It's bad for business, having someone like him in full view of your customers," she said to Mom.

"Ben's a good man," Mom told Mrs. Finkle. "He's having a bit of a rough time and needs a little help right now."

That was the end of the conversation. Mom thanked Mrs. Finkle for her grocery purchases and went back to filling holes in the cigarette stand with packages of Marlboro, Winston, and Camel, still with a smile on her face, the same kind joy in her eyes.

Then there was Mrs. Hawkins, the red-haired devil with the nasty attitude and a live-in boyfriend. At the age of seventy-five, she was the talk of the neighborhood, but Mom treated her kindly, with as much respect as she gave everyone. When voices tittered and rumors flew, my mother would ignore them and advised us to do the same.

"We have no right to judge," she would say. "Remember the old adage, 'Never judge a person unless you've walked a mile in their shoes.'"

Somehow, this knowledge evaded us. Midst the flaming red hair, being squirted with cold water from the hose if we walked too close to her lawn, and her refusal to answer our knocks on Halloween nights, stories grew and the imaginations of local children sprouted wings. Mrs. Hawkins was a witch. She held children prisoner in her basement. She ate worms and raised poisonous plants in her garden.

So my sisters and I found ourselves in the alley behind her house that day. Her car was there. The trunk was open. It had been a lovely fall and the sycamore trees had dumped a grand load of leaves, all brown and gold and crinkly. We could hear Mrs. Hawkins in her house, banging and swearing and probably doing worse things.

We swung into action, grabbing handfuls of leaves and stuffing them into her trunk. Pride swelled in my chest and I imagined myself vindicating the mistreatment of all the children she had imprisoned over the years. Just as we were finished and the trunk was overflowing, Mrs. Hawkins came at us, broom in hand. She chased us up the street, but we were quick. Through the store we ran, out the back door, into our house, up the stairs. We dove under our beds. All was quiet. So quiet.

"Not my girls," Mom told Mrs. Hawkins. "They would never."

As Mrs. Hawkins prattled on, our rapid flight through the store began to make sense, and Mom recanted: "They're hardly vandals. When you calm down, I'm sure you'll realize. They do, however, owe you an apology."

Mom relayed the story calmly, minutes later. She prodded us with a soft, "come on now," and we crawled from under our beds. She sat in a chair with a dictionary in her hand. "Vandalism," she read, "means willful or malicious destruction of public or private property." My sisters and I sat cross-legged on my bed facing her. Heads down, we accepted our lesson in crime and punishment.

We followed Mom downstairs, out the back door, and up the alley to Mrs. Hawkins's car. She watched while my sisters and I emptied the trunk of every leaf and leaf skeleton, depositing them neatly beside the sycamore tree that had dropped them. "Sorry," I told Mrs. Hawkins, mouth in a grimace. "Sorry," my younger sisters whispered, following my lead.

All my life, I never heard my mother raise her voice. I never heard her yell at my father, nor he at her. I could hear discussions from their bedroom late at night, words that came through the walls like feathers of thought, but it was never anything more than a comfort to my ears. Their tenderness transferred to us, three girls who never had an occasion to learn how to fight.

Though challenged by growing up and the paths through life I chose, my mother's voice in my head never faltered. Her words were there when I fell in love for the first time. Her message was clear as I marched in protest of the Vietnam War and ran through the 1960s with a pride of conviction I learned early on from her. My mother's warnings about safe boundaries were clear as I tested the waters of freedom as a young adult, married, and had children of my own. From Mom I learned how to be a mother. I knew that the most important things to teach my sons were that family comes first; that we must respect each other's feelings; appreciate our likenesses and differences; and that we must treat others as we wanted to be treated ourselves.

I see my mother now as a revolutionary. Her empathy toward those less fortunate and visions of equality among all peoples were, in the 1950s, astounding. At eighty-four, she is still an inspiration. She remains true to herself and what she taught my sisters and me.

Today my friend brought homemade chocolate pudding to work. She called it "chocolate gravy" and said the recipe had deep roots, stemming from her mother-in-law via an old family tradition. Luisa warmed the "gravy" in the microwave and the smell was intoxicating. It put me in the mood to talk with Mom, to tell her that I take joy in remembering what it felt like to run across a lawn covered by fall leaves at night, to help Dad close up the store: turn off the lights, shut the lids on the refrigeration units, cover the fruit and vegetables with a heavy cloth tarp, lock the door, count and stash the money, to feel proud and part of something important.

The smell of chocolate made me think of lying in bed with my parents on Wednesday nights, family night, story night, and of Mom telling us about how it was to grow up during the Depression in Filer, Idaho—stories about our ancestors, a lack of acceptance for my great-grandparents, a young Cherokee couple recently moved there from Oklahoma. "The folks in town teased Grandpa and called him *Squawman*," she told us sadly. "Babe, your great-grandmother was ignored by local women and she couldn't buy groceries in the general store."

Without her telling me, I realized how those truths had shaped my mother's life.

Chocolate pudding was a luxury when my mother was growing up. For my sisters and me, it was a gift, a sign of the richness of our family and the loving spirit of our home. I am humbled by and proud of my mother today and grateful for the simple gifts she gave and continues to give everyone she touches. In these difficult times when heroes are hard to come by, I need only to look at her.

My son told me recently that it is important to *pay it forward*, to give to others when you have been blessed. Helping others is inborn for him. Kindness and generosity are hand-me-downs. In him I see my mother's soul.

These days Mom and I laugh about the shenanigans my sisters and I pulled when we were children and our experience with Mrs. Hawkins.

"And you loved me still?" I ask her for the millionth time. "Even after that?"

"Even then," says Mom, eyes aglow with tears.

Quiet Morsels with My Mum

Rebecca Milford

She had said the changing rooms were too hot, the layers of fleece and scarf were stifling, and she'd meet me at the air-conditioned counter where jewelry dangled like glistening hooks for passing fish. I found out later that she actually just couldn't bear the sight of my bony shoulders protruding through the various fabrics I was trying on.

After the birthday shopping was complete, we headed to a little cafe nearby for a drink. The ancient cathedral spire of Bath stretched up into the slate-gray sky and the cobbled streets resounded with excited chatter of tourists. The teashop, nestled in an alcove just off the main square, was alive with the clatter of visitors' forks and the china clink of cups and saucers.

I declined Mum's suggestion of cake. I'd become adept at casually waving away offers of food, and instead insisted I wanted a green tea. We had a stilted conversation about my upcoming birthday, how she was getting along teaching the kids at college. How I was enjoying London. What my brother was getting up to.

She sat and nodded, her sm ile painted with one of the many rose lipsticks I'd chosen over the years for Christmas presents, bringing the cappuccino up slowly to take careful sips. Every so often her gray eyes travelled to my cup of hot water and skeletal wrists that seemed barely able to lift the mug, a green pattern on cheap china. Blue veins snaking visibly under paper-pale skin. Once she sighed, and I shifted in my seat, my gaze beginning to wander outside. I had become fidgety and inattentive. When things seemed strained, which they constantly were now, I became irritable. Strange, to not want the obvious mentioned, but to feel a crushing suffocation when normality was pretended.

It had become like living a half-life, constantly moving through dusk, terribly lonely. I couldn't be around food, the smell of bacon sandwiches or the trays of carefully iced cakes and buns, oozing chocolate or resplendent with berries and treacle. I pecked Mum on the cheek and told her I'd see her at home tomorrow for my birthday tea. Retreating into the chilly air, I left her staring helplessly into the empty coffee cup.

Rebecca and her mum, 2010

We'd had a tempestuous relationship when I was growing through my teens. In those situations people often suggest a mother and daughter are just too similar. I don't know how much accuracy there was in this, apart from the fact we'd both scream at one another but, deep down, were scared by our own shouts. She'd retreat into herself, hunch fuming and shaking over the sink, while I slammed doors and wept hot, angry tears into my pillow.

When I went to university it got better. We respected each other and I found the love I'd always had for her had grown into a desperate protection. I wanted more than anything for her to be happy, knowing I needed her for security more than any other person alive. There is something wonderfully terrifying about smelling her skin-warmed perfume as I cuddle into her, feeling more comforted than I thought possible, always aware that one day the passing scent of it on a spring afternoon will be devastating and cause me to crumble like a sand castle assaulted by the tide.

We have a small family, five of us in all, and each fits perfectly into this precious collection. And so we were assembled on my birthday afternoon as I turned twenty-four. My hippy father, who had been too flighty for my practical mother. Yet they remained such close friends that neither had found a new partner. Sam, my brother, was still living at home and equally protective over Mum.

And there was Granny, navigating the wrapping paper strewn across the floor, bringing the birthday cake into the low-lit room as candles flickered, so I could blow out the dancing flames. Pale pink icing glazed the cake's surface, and a tiny figurine of a ballerina pirouetted across its unblemished surface. *Happy Birthday Becca* spelled out in silver balls. A labor of love. Victoria sandwich, my favorite.

Of course I refused my slice. Every morsel now had a value in my head—my brain would whir, unforced, into a calorie calculator that spun like a pin-machine—jam, sponge, sugar—the fat involved! One slice was unimaginable. How could people sit and chew on the slices of light, fluffy cake and then lick the crumbs from their plate? I was already aware I had accepted full-fat milk in my tea rather than the usual skimmed—Mum refused to buy it.

So the arguments started. Not shouts anymore—no pleas. Just exasperation from my dad—did I not see what I was doing? I was killing myself. My organs were failing. Susan, you agree don't you? Of course, Christopher, but what can I say? Open palms and unintended blame while I sat, fuming that a stupid thing like beaten butter and sugar and egg should be the cause of such disharmony. It was the fault of the birthday cake. Mum turned to me helplessly—I shook my head, warning her, and she knew I'd leave. So she shrugged and was defeated, and we made a sad effort at playing a board game.

Things came to a head when I visited my auntie—actually my mum's best friend—in France. She was shocked at my six-stone frame and collarbones that jutted out like cuttlefish-bones or the ridge of spine that stood out from my wasted back. I had always enjoyed these visits, trips to the *Cafe de la Pays* for fish soup or the local pizzeria where we'd share anchovy and chorizo slices. Now I pushed lettuce around my plate and the prospect of going for meals terrified me—would I be forced to eat certain things? How much could I leave without causing offence? I would feign sleep to avoid the home-cooked meals of *confit de canard* or fatty *pâté*.

My auntie mentioned it, but I insisted I was fine. She phoned my mum in shock— how could she let this happen to her daughter? When I returned to England, I received an email saying it wouldn't be wise for me to go out there again—it was too painful for my aunt. I was anorexic and I couldn't see it—something the doctors had suggested but my family had never actually mentioned. They'd say I was too thin, but the actual word hadn't come up. It seemed too clinical. I wasn't sick; I was careful. I simply tried to live on less than 500 calories a day and enjoyed exercising excessively.

Not long afterwards Mum invited me out for lunch—she had a two-for-one voucher. Normally, I would have shrunk from the idea, like a subterranean creature avoiding sunlight, but something in her voice was cracked and sounded desperate. We went to the restaurant and I ordered a prawn salad with no dressing. My mum looked at the menu and said she'd have the same.

We chatted about what I was writing at the moment and how she was getting along with the book I'd lent her. We laughed about my granny and her tales of the neighbors. We'd never really spent time like this before. I no longer lived in Bath and when I did visit, it was a hasty coffee snatched between her lectures and my meetings with friends. Now it was just the two of us, as adults, for one of the first times in my life.

And so the food arrived, and I pushed it about on my plate a bit and began to talk, animated and overlively, filling the time with words and gulps of water so I could avoid taking bites. Mum nodded, listened, and then told her own story. Without thinking, I speared a piece of cucumber and ate it. She did the same, mirroring my movements exactly. Conversation flowed surprisingly easily, without the arguments I'd come to expect or the comments on my weight.

Dad had tried various tactics, all of which were useless. If he tried to be supportive and tell me I was looking healthier, then I took it as meaning I was getting heavier and fatter and would retreat into an outraged sulk. Then when he insisted I eat anything because I was stick-thin, I'd feel a glow of pride and become more determined.

But Mum and I just talked, like friends tentatively catching up after a long time. Every time I took a bite she would, too. It was turning into a long meal and my stomach was rumbling after too long with food in front of me—normally the other diner would have finished by now and the plates would be cleared. But her food disappeared at the same pace. I tried my tactic of insisting she try some of mine; to my friends I was an acknowledged "feeder."

It was difficult to try this ploy since she had the same meal and cleverly deflected the morsel back onto my plate. It was frustrating, and yet somehow comforting. Time ticked along and I felt guilty about the amount of food remaining on her plate. Then suddenly, on taking a mouthful of prawn, I realized I was mirroring her action of putting the fork to her lips. When we finally left there were two virtually untouched plates, and yet I'd eaten more than I had in months.

I was going back to London that afternoon, and she walked me to the train station. I didn't feel the usual guilt at having food, just a strange, sad little depression in the pit of my stomach. There was something so feeble about it. When she said good-bye, she hugged me tight, and I felt her hands run over the sharp blades of my shoulder. I breathed in her perfume.

"Oh, Becca," she said softly, because the words were choked, "I just want my little girl back." I got on the train and waved to her from my seat, my vision blurry and helpless. When I reached into my bag to get my phone, my fingers brushed something soft, a little hare teddy. Her nickname for me.

I returned to Bath a month later and invited her to lunch. It was as painful to suggest it as I'd expected. I was heavier by half a stone, and I was sure this would be like an admission I was now eating like any normal, fat person. I waited for the joyous announcements that I was looking better, heavier, healthier, all of which brought hot pricks to my eyes. But Mum didn't say anything. We hugged and went in for another long lunch—identical mouthfuls and identical bites, but by the end of the meal there was a little less to clear away.

And so every time I return home we go for a meal. Sometimes there is more left on the plate than at others. Last time I ordered chicken rather than a fish salad, and we both left the potatoes. Our mirrored meals have made us so much closer, not only because we talk about life and silly things. Each time we meet our bond strengthens. I am learning to understand myself, and what it means to have a problem. Mum knew that I would not be shouted down, but that a little hare teddy in my bag and a silent, gentle battle every time we eat together would reach me. That is why I am getting better, and she is the reason for this.

Liebestraum: A Daughter's Reflection

Jeanne Jusaitis

*H*er hands drop tentatively, softly, on the keys of our old player piano, and I recognize the opening chords of "Liebestraum." My mother plays on, but with more confidence so that the music crescendos just where it should. My thirteen-year-old chest aches for my mother, for her tenderness, her beauty. It is only when she plays this song, the song that means love's dream, that I see the melancholy.

She turns to me with a big smile, giving up on the piece. "I wish I could play that like my mother," she says. Light from the afternoon sun streams through the window to brighten her auburn hair.

"I like the way you play it," I say. "Nana does better with the jazzy pieces."

Mom smiles. "She plays by ear you know." She starts "Liebestraum" again, reading the music this time.

Later, as an adult, I watched her play, wondering where the sadness came from and why she never took credit for what she did well.

People have described my mother as pretty, kind, and always a lady. Never wanting to attract attention, she was the 1950s television mom. She didn't wear high heels when she vacuumed, but she did wear white canvas Keds. She was our room mother, my Camp Fire leader. She made extra money by making everyone's costumes for the Christmas pageant, starting every June. My sister and I took ballet classes with the money she earned.

During my elementary school years, there didn't seem to be an aspect of my life where she wasn't involved, and I sometimes resented that. She volunteered for Red Cross. She played Bridge with "the girls." Although she was a member of the Women's Club and Eastern Star, few people knew of her background. They knew she was a city girl, new to the tiny northern California town of Crockett as of 1940, but they didn't really know . . .

Once in the late forties, when I was about four, she stood behind me and brushed my hair while I recited a little poem that I'd learned from my friends on the sidewalk. Eeny, meeny, miney, mo . . . When I said the "n" word, my mother hit me with the hairbrush. She never did that before or since. I had no idea what the word meant or why it was so bad.

Jeanne's mom, age 69, at wedding of Jeanne's sister

She said, "Do you like the man who always helps Nana at the train station?"

"Yes," I said. "He looks just like Pinky Marie's daddy." *Pinky Marie* was my favorite book.

"Well, you'd be hurting his feelings, saying that poem. I don't want to hear that word again."

I think that was the first time I felt shame. I promised her I wouldn't repeat that word, but still couldn't get over the fact that she had hit me with those gentle loving hands . . . the same hands that felt my forehead for a temperature, rubbed my back and played "Liebestraum." Where did her sudden anger come from?

My mother's sparkling eyes usually accompanied an easy smile, a ready laugh. She'd roll out the dough for a lemon me-ringue pie, teach me to deal cards, or hold my hands as we danced around the living room to a 78 record—she always found ways for us to have fun. On rainy days, my sister and I would make a rhythm band out of her pots and pans and parade around the house. The noise didn't bother her. She'd throw a blanket over a card table and we'd make a fort. At bedtime she'd sing us songs in her low, sweet voice and tell us nursery stories and fairy tales. She was the mom all my friends wanted, so upbeat, so understanding.

And then I remember the parts of my mother that I know, that I've seen, that maybe nobody else has. There's the blue flash of anger in her eye when she speaks of the circumstances of her parent's divorce, of her stepfather's violence, of her hardworking mother. I've heard the sadness in her voice when she talked of protecting her little brother and stepsister. And then there's that picture of an old boyfriend named Earle. It lay in the bottom of her blanket chest. Was she thinking of any of them as she played the achingly lovely notes of "Liebestraum?"

Maybe it was none of those things. Maybe the big ideas were what made her sad—injustice, small-mindedness, and poverty.

As a child, my mother was a daredevil. She lived in Seattle, at the edge of Lake Washington where she found all kinds of ways to have fun. She would try any kind of acrobatic feat, including a flip off the roof of a barn. She'd roll down the steep hills in a go-cart with no brakes. She almost drowned when she fell into a huge pickle barrel in the back of her parent's butter and eggs store at Pikes Pier. Her younger years were idyllic until her own immediate family fell apart due to the Depression and her father's meanderings. Her mother, my Nana Mae, sent her across country on a train at the age of nine to chaperone her little brother. She attended eleven different schools.

A few years later, my grandfather sent his wife and two children to San Francisco. Mae was a pianist in jazz clubs and would take on any kind of menial day job to support her two children. In San Francisco, the three of them lived in a garage with a dirt floor and orange crates for furniture. When they finally got a small apartment, Mom and her brother slept in a big drawer-bed.

They'd peek through the cracks around the drawer-bed to watch the parties her flamboyant mother threw after the clubs closed. Black and white artists and musicians of all nationalities would come to after-work parties at her house to jam with her charismatic mother who held court from the piano stool. My grandmother's personality and joviality filled a room and drew people in. She loved being the center of attention. My mother adored her. When there were enough donations to pay for somebody's rent, they'd party on, into the morning hours, for the joy of it. I'm sure that Mom and her little brother saw all kinds of behaviors that she kept to herself. She had so many secrets. My father always called her his mystery woman.

Her teenage years were not carefree. Through diligence and a serious work ethic in school and in various jobs, my mother brought herself and her little brother up through her mother's second marriage and more turmoil. She stayed in favor with her troublesome father while she was at war with her alcoholic stepfather.

In reflection, I am impressed by her resilience, her ability to rise above her circumstances, but I can understand why she was determined to give my sister and me the perfect family life that she didn't have, the dance classes she didn't have, the mother she didn't have.

What a change it must have been for her to be swept up into the security of my father's gang of friends. They lived in San Francisco, had country houses in Marin County, rode around in jalopies, and went to dances at the Y. I've studied her black leather scrapbook full of photos of those times. White calligraphy from my father's pen labels the pictures mounted on black paper: *Pyramid at Neptune Beach, Bathing Beauties at Samuel P. Taylor, Mugging at Sutro's Baths.*

My parents married when my mother had just turned nineteen. My father was hired as a director at the 1939 World's Fair and they both entered a year of colored lights and ferry rides. Mom put herself through secretarial school and worked at Atlas Heating. Frugal to a fault, she put money away for the future and rescued her mother and brother from time to time. When my father secured a teaching job in a small town north of San Francisco, she was apprehensive. She didn't know how to drive. She'd never been far from her mother. She'd never known the small minds of a small town. She never would have guessed that she'd spend the rest of her life there.

Many years later, as she sat at the piano in our beautiful mid-century house on the hill, I held back tears for her; tears for her struggle, her secret wishes I felt none of us could fulfill. Was she really happy? Had she just settled? Had her work been enough? Had we been enough? Her "Liebestraum" told me how much she loved us, but I wondered if she felt lonely.

In the late fifties, when I started high school, Mom went to work. She was given a position with the Federal Housing Authority that allowed her to find homes for the poor, stand up for the weak, and, on her own, find jobs for those willing to work. It was many years later that I realized the influence her passions and beliefs had played out in my own teaching career— supporting the underdog, teaching tolerance.

As I entered high school, Mom went back to school and got the credentials to become the manager of a federal housing project in north Richmond and then, later, in Rodeo. She truly cared and looked out for the families she came to know. Her mostly African-American Richmond project was bigger than our entire little white northern California town of Crockett.

In 1961, when I was sixteen, my mother encouraged me to enter an essay contest, the topic being civil rights. I won a trip to an American Friends Conference where I spent inspirational hours sitting with the young Martin Luther King Jr. and six other students, black and white, on the sand dunes of Asilomar, a conference center on California's scenic Monterey Peninsula. We talked about our fears and prejudices. We talked of our cities and high schools. We talked about change and how we could help it along. I could feel my mother's smile of approval all the way from home. At night, we'd sit around the beach fire and sing "We Shall Overcome" and "Blowin' in the Wind." I came back to Crockett ready to change the world, and if not, at least mix it up a little at my high school. I had a plan.

A few months later, Mom stood at her bathroom sink, dabbing her favorite scent, Wicked Wahine, behind her ears. I think that she enjoyed the name of that perfume because it made her feel daring, wicked.

"Mom," I said. "Would it be okay if I invited some of the Prom Committee to our house to make decorations? I was thinking next Saturday."

"I'm taking your sister to ballet in the morning, but you could have them over later, in the afternoon." A definite pause. "Did you manage to get some of the girls from the Project on your committee?"

"Yes, three of them." I said. "You know what? It's the first time any of the black kids have been on a committee. I had a hard time talking Doris into it. Then Doris asked two more girls, and they said they'd be on the committee, but they act like they don't want to come here. I just can't think of anyplace else, and school's closed on Saturdays."

"I know their parents. Let me talk to them," she said.

Some of Mom's magic? In a few days the girls were on board and planning to come to my house to make paper flowers. Moonlight and Roses—that was our theme. There were seven or eight of us on the committee. None of the Crockett girls had ever been in a private home with Negroes and whites together. We were a little nervous, but also excited by our boldness and by the opportunity to get to know each other. The Project was in another town, so Doris's mother, Mrs. Daniels, would drive the girls up to our house.

Saturday came, and Mrs. Daniels delivered the girls. Mom went out to the car wearing her apron and invited her in, but Doris's mother said that she was busy and would be back later to pick them up.

In hindsight, it was a historic day, and I'll never forget how my mother got such joy out of shocking the neighbors, who peeked out from behind their curtains with judging lips and curious eyes. "That'll get their tongues wagging," she laughed with a gleam in her eye.

The day was a huge success. The Prom Committee sat on the floor in front of the fireplace making crepe paper flowers, playing hit parade records, and gossiping about everybody we could think of. When Mrs. Daniels came back to pick up the girls, we couldn't believe the time. We had broken some old barriers. It wasn't until many years later that I realized the impact at the high school, and that it all started with my mom.

In 1995, her funeral was held in Crockett. I was surprised to see several people from the Projects. She had been retired for ten years. So many told me that my mother had helped them get an apartment, or a job, or had helped them out in some other way. Seldom did she talk about these things, she just did them. She was a humble person. It was so important for her to give people their privacy, their dignity. They never forgot.

In retrospect, I can see that my grandmother's legacy of love, determination, music and laughter came through my mother to me. I am impressed by the way my mother was able to bow to the narrow conventions of a wife and mother's role of the 1950s and '60s while maintaining a career and independent views. Those early years, the Depression years, scarred her in ways I'll never know, but I do know that her trials made her strong. Yet, somehow, there lurked, deep in my mom, something lonely and wistful. That's what I heard in her "Liebestraum."

I am humbled by the gifts I've received from my mother's sacrifices, her love of family, and the hard lessons she learned growing up. My first degree in Fine Arts stemmed from the passion for music and dance that she passed down to me. As a classroom teacher, the love and understanding that I showed for my students came from my mother's need to help people and to respect the dignity of others. Her strong sense of independence and pride gave me the courage to find new ways to teach and to keep growing.

Recently, I watched an ice-skater glide effortlessly across the blue ice of my flat screen television set, her diaphanous white dress in contrast to the black void around her. She skated to "Liebestraum." I thought that I picked up the faint scent of Wicked Wahine, then wept, missing my mother's love.

Motherless Moments

Danielle Christopher

I inhale the dry air as I whip around the corner ready to try the jump again. My cheeks burn from the speed and the chill off the ice. I lift into the jump, certain that it is a good one, and land on both feet. Dang. I berate myself as I hear the booming voice of my coach, "Start over."

I feel my mother's warm smile beaming from the viewing area. It's like she is right beside me whispering in my ear, "Just have fun." One glance toward the speaker that bellows out my music, and I smile, straighten my shoulders, and wait for the beat to begin. Then one crisp glide to the first spin, and I am off.

I am fueled by the power and motivation that I will make this double salchow. I have to do it. There is no point in my competing if I can't do the jump that gives me higher points. Here I go, up and away. Halfway through, I think about the land and feel that I will not make it; I land on two feet again. I don't need my coach to tell me how bad that landing was. I ignore him and continue the routine.

I love figure skating, but I am not competitive. My family is filled with figure skaters. My maternal grandpa and my mother were active skaters at the local skating clubs back in Vancouver near my hometown. When I showed interest, at four years old, they jumped me into lessons with really no pressure to compete because they just enjoyed it. I know I can, too.

The momentum steers me around the corner toward the viewing area where all the moms, grandparents, and other spectators are watching today's practice. I look up and catch my mom's eye. Her smile warms the chill. Seeing her bright smile light up as our eyes meet reminds me of the talk we had right before practice—if I am nervous, don't be. "Just have fun."

Later, on Christmas Eve, I get out of my bed carefully. I tiptoe to my door and open it a crack. I sit by the floor ready to jump into bed if I hear my parents come down the hall. I can hear them watching television at the other end of the house. I barely allow myself to breathe. I hope they go to bed soon so Santa can come; I am wide-awake in anticipation of seeing Santa.

After about an hour, my parents shut off the television. Finally, I think. They need to go to bed! Only they don't—I hear lights being turned on and furniture being moved. I go down on

Danielle and her mother, 1981, last picture before mother's cancer returned

my belly, trying to peer down the hall into the living room to see what is going on. Then I hear my mother.

"I'm tired. We should get the stuff out. Do you want the cookie?" she asks my dad.

His reply is muffled by the sound of paper rustling and a box being ripped open. I can't take it anymore so I open my door and creep down the hallway to get a better look. My heart stops when I see the Barbie Dream House I've begged for, being built by my dad. Packing materials are strewn everywhere. I almost speak up when I hear my sister moving in her room, which is next to where I am standing.

I race back into my bed and pull the covers over my head. I wonder if Santa didn't have time to deliver and put together the house, so he left it for my dad. With a jolt, I realize that the neighborhood kids are right. There is no Santa. It is our parents who build the fantasy. Before I can think any more sad thoughts, I fall asleep.

When school is out for the summer, I am allowed to stay up a little later than usual. I've always loved my bedtime routine with my mom, my right foot dangling in the green shag carpet with my left tucked under my right leg. I am snug in my mother's lap on our black vinyl recliner in the living room. Her arms are wrapped around me like a seat belt. We say our "good nights." As I pad off down the hallway to my bedroom, she calls to me, "Wait." I turn around with a grin. I know what's next.

"I love you more than a million oceans," she says.

"I love you more than a million oceans, too." I blow her a kiss. I hit the pillow in my Star Wars-sheeted bed unaware that it will be the last night we spend together in the same house.

I awake the next day to spend two weeks with my maternal grandparents in Manitoba, flying for the first time. My grandpa, grandma, and I will be visiting my grandpa's family. Unbeknown to me, my mom is going into the hospital for the last time. She had been in and out of the hospital many times and at their home cancer was whispered. Sometimes I saw my grandparents wipe away tears from their faces when I entered a room. I never understood. My mom died of breast cancer a week after I got back from the trip.

Years later I am in the viewing area of the local gymnasium watching my three-year-old going through her routine. She does not land correctly on every jump or complete her rolls, but she is laughing and smiling at the teacher. Just this morning, I told her the same thing my mother told me all those years ago. When the fun stops, we'll find something new that is. Something tells me today is not the last day in the gym.

Before I know it, I am planning our Christmas list and budget. I wonder how my parents did it. I manage to sneak a lot of gifts into the house. It is part of the Mom job I love.

"Mommy." Before I crack an eye open my three year old daughter smothers me in kisses. She bounces over to her daddy who is pretending to be sleeping.

"It's Christmas. Santa came. Let's go!" she demands.

"Keep it down. You will wake your sister," I request, too late. All the family is up now.

We go downstairs to the living room together. I smile at the memory I had about that last Christmas I spent with my mom. I never did tell her I found out Santa wasn't real, but the looks on my children's faces makes me believe in Santa's magic.

It has been twenty-six years since my mom died and I still miss her, especially at the holidays. I remember her sitting in the black vinyl chair, cane at her side, smiling at us enjoying the Christmas presents. Each day is hard, and easy, all at once. I give myself permission to embrace my grief that my children did not have their grandma and I feel lighter. By letting go, I can begin to tell my daughters my stories of when I was a kid. Showing them pictures reminds me of the happy times. I do things that remind me of Mom, like watching her favorite Christmas movie and enjoying her special coffee. She will always be a part of my heart and soul.

My youngest toddles over to me with her new Elmo toy. She gives it a big hug and joins her sister back on the floor. I take a deep sip of my coffee with Baileys, just like Mom. I feel the warmth of the holidays and the knowledge that my daughters know their grandma through my stories and pictures of my childhood. I take great comfort in that.

The following month, I see my darling daughter searching for me across the gym. Our eyes connect and we share a warm smile. She bounces off to the high bar. Within minutes the class is gathered for the wrap-up song and then the door opens. I hold my arms out to welcome my little acrobat. I ask her if she had fun. She replies with a big "YES!"

I put her shoes on her, and we head out the door to the car. I only had my mother for the first ten years of my life, and I never appreciated her mothering gifts until I became a mom. She never was a great housekeeper or cook, but she gave me a great gift. Unconditional love is the best gift I could have received from her. We have a lot more in common than I realized until becoming a mom myself. I smile as we pull away in the car. Knowing that I parent like my mother makes me feel closer to her.

On one hard day, I am fighting not to cry in front of the kids. The lonely ache of missing my mom overwhelms me so much I can barely breathe. The whir of the dishwasher drowns out the loud shouting from the kids who are playing eight feet away in the playroom. The townhouse is big. It has three floors, but today it feels like a shoebox. It's supposed to be quiet time, and my youngest is due for her nap soon. But by the sounds in the next room, it will be hard to slow my girls down.

I really could use my mom today. The hours fly by in a sleep-deprived diaper haze since my husband left for work. My three-year-old is a tiny tornado, and my nineteen-month-old is miserable teething. The rain pelting on the roof makes me wonder if it will cave in. The weather cancels our plans to go to a park, which is their favorite thing to do. Just the idea of packing them up to go to a mall or the library is exhausting. On top of everything, I have to pee so badly, I finally put my screaming baby down on the bathroom floor while I go.

There is no one I can call to rescue me for even an hour. In my small village, towns away from where I grew up, those who could help are working the same hours as my husband. All my mommy friends have gone back to work since their maternity leaves have ended. I feel lonely, but never alone.

I am washing my hands at the bathroom sink when a little head bumps me in my behind—my toddler gesturing to be picked up. I scoop her up and she gives me the biggest hug ever. At that same moment, my oldest runs up to me and hugs my legs, telling me I am her best friend. Swallowing the pity that bubbles in my throat, I kneel on the floor to hug them both at the same time.

Their unconditional love for me reminds me that while I do not have my mom, my girls still need theirs.

Later that night, "I got it," my three year old daughter bellows and brings me a book for story time, Bedtime Rhymes. We snuggle into our blue fabric chair (which does not recline) in our living room, lit by the reading lamp over our shoulders.

I read the book twice and hug her tight. I do not want to let go.

"Goodnight, sweetheart. I love you more than a million oceans." I give her a kiss.

"I know, Mom. I love you, too," she says as we climb the stairs to her bedroom.

I settle her into her bed. She closes her eyes.

My mother was not able to tell me much about life before she died. I have no idea what she wanted me to become. I do not know if she breast-fed me or if I was what she wanted in a child. What is locked in my heart is that I know she loved me. She told me many times a day with affection. The best a mom can do is listen to and love her children as if they are the most important people in the world. My mom did and it is how I parent. Love lessons are worth more than a million oceans. I didn't know how to parent when I became pregnant. I panicked. I am not a great cook or housekeeper, but I love my children more than anything. All I could do, and still do, is love them with all my heart. Just like my mom always did

As much as I miss my mom, I realize that there were many moments that make up my memories of her. I can't recall a bad time except for her funeral. I try to not focus on those bad moments. I hold onto all the positive ones in my heart. My daughters will not remember that I bake cookies from a package—they will remember all the moments we create as we live them. Moment by moment is what we have right now, filled with love.

The Bed

Diane Hurles

*M*y mother's illness defined my childhood from the time I was seven years old. My older brother, Nick, younger sister, Sue, and I were protected as children. No one ever told us what was really wrong. Cancer was a synonym for death back in the 1960s, so we were told Mom had a "bone disease" and I never thought to question it. There wasn't a moment I didn't believe she'd get well. "When Mom gets better" was our family's mantra, the only timeline we knew.

Only when I was in college did I learn that Mom had breast cancer. In the shower one morning she had found a lump the size of a pea and soon it had invaded her bones, more specifically her spine. For most of her illness she spent her days in a full-sized hospital bed set up in the middle of our dining room. When I think about Mom, that's how I remember her most—propped up in bed, her dark hair in small pigtails so it wouldn't snarl, with a lime-green wooden bed tray placed in front of her. She ate from that tray, wrote from that tray, and used it to rest her knitting needles and embroidery hoops when she was in the middle of creating a sweater or a cross-stitch sampler.

"Diane, come help me," Mom would yell, and I knew exactly what she wanted me to do: sit next to her bed and hold my arms up in front me so she could drape a new skein of yarn over them and roll it up in a ball for her latest project. I didn't catch on then, but she used those quiet moments, time that usually made me restless, to check in with me, go over my homework, and ask me about my day.

Her bed had a mattress that you could move up and down with a remote control and we used to climb in and "ride" the bed with her. I loved to lie in between the pink-flowered sheets that were Mom's favorites and try out the different mattress positions. Head up, feet down. Head down, feet up. But never both head and feet up at the same time, "the pretzel" we called it, unless Mom happened to be sitting up in her wheelchair and we had the bed to ourselves. I learned early on that, in the cozy confines of her bed, even when I was doing nothing more than holding that skein of yarn, I had

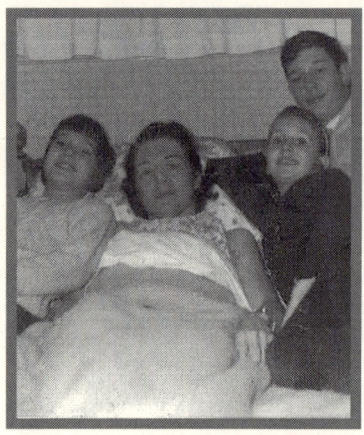

Diane (left) and her siblings sharing the bed with Mom

to be careful not to get too close, or be too rambunctious, always mindful of how fragile she was. Still, she'd encourage us to join her under the covers on her good days, and I competed with my little sister to see who would get to lie next to her.

One weekend afternoon Mom and I heard a knock at the front door and she asked me to go see who it was.

"Are your parents home?" the man on the front stoop asked me. I had never seen him before, but I imagine Mom recognized his voice—or expected his visit—because she called out to me to let him in. I opened the door and watched as he followed her voice into the dining room. Then, as soon as he got there, he stopped. Blatantly. Abruptly. As if his legs had brakes. Oh, I thought, he's never been here before. In front of him was not the china-filled hutch and table and chairs he probably expected, but Mom lying in bed, tucked warmly under the covers, with the pillows around her both supporting and comforting her delicate body.

"Don't worry; I'm not contagious," she told him, smiling, trying to put him at ease. "I have a bad back." Within a few minutes Mom charmed him into conversation and his uneasiness waned. Even so, I felt sorry for the man. Sorry he was caught by surprise. I should have told him not to be scared of the bed.

Mom couldn't walk without relying on a walker and a big metal back brace with thick beige straps that looked heavy and uncomfortable. It made her torso look too big for the rest of her body.

"How did I get so wide?" she once remarked to no one in particular while giving herself a once-over in the mirror. A star drum majorette in high school and former Ottawa County Peach Queen, she noticed in detail how her weakening body was conforming to the illness. She was shorter; her hair was thinner. Her medication made her develop small tufts of facial hair, which I overheard her complain about to Dad. Looking at her in bed, her fragile, bone-thin arms covered by one of the many frumpy bed jackets she received from friends, it was hard for me to imagine her beauty queen days. I felt sad, knowing how anxious she must be to get better and become that person again. Getting better, I thought, would magically transform her body, so cocooned by the frustrations of her illness, into the butterfly I knew she missed so desperately.

Hospital stays became routine for Mom throughout her treatment and, as much as I missed her, I always dreaded visitation days because I wasn't old enough to go up to her room. Hospital rules said you had to be twelve. Most often Dad would bring her down to the lobby in a wheelchair where we were waiting. But sometimes we would beat the system and the nurses, oozing with compassion for two scared young girls, would sneak Sue and me up the back stairwell, reassuring us all the way that it was okay.

"Your mom's been talking about your coming all morning," they'd say.

Still, it felt awkward and wrong. I'm sure I tried to hop in bed for a ride once we got up to her room, probably more than once, but quickly learned their compassion had limits.

"Careful, honey. Your mom's had a rough morning," the nurse would warn protectively, no doubt referring to the bouts of nausea that often accompanied the mega doses of medicine she received in the hospital.

"Don't listen to them," Mom would respond with a laugh.

But, embarrassed, I'd shrug it off with a quick, "That's okay," and lean against the wall or stand by the door for the rest of the visit, anxious to get going.

When she was home, Mom was often groggy from pain medication and there were many times when I'd settle in next to her on the bed to watch television, only to have her fall asleep during the good parts. It frustrated me, but I still cherished those television times when we'd watch *The King Family* or *Lawrence Welk* on a small black-and-white set that was suspended from the ceiling so she could see the screen comfortably from the bed. I don't remember watching much drama, or even comedy for that matter, just happy, upbeat singers. There was a comfort to the music that matched the comfort of the bed.

Stretched out in my pajamas next to Mom, the pillows fluffed up, while watching those impossibly perky singers singing wholesome songs with lipstick-bright smiles on their faces, gave me some of the greatest sense of security I remember having as a child. For an hour or two I was living in their world, where everything was perfect, thinking ahead to the day when my world would be perfect, too. Everything will be okay, those singers were telling me. And I believed them.

Most times, though, away from the television and the bedcovers, I felt anything but secure. With Mom's sickness came the constant concern and sympathy of others, pity that filled me with an almost tangible self-consciousness, as if I were walking around with a big asterisk over my head.

*She's different.

*Poor thing.

*Be nice.

I was embarrassed because my family was different. I was uncomfortable because people singled us out. All I really wanted to feel was normal. More than anything, I wanted to feel normal.

"Normal" to me back then meant being able to do family things on the spur of the moment. It meant blending in at school. And it meant having the kind of house my friends had with new furniture and plush carpet. A house kept neat enough for us to invite people over on a whim. Especially one that didn't have a bed in the dining room. But the closest I remember we ever got to new furniture after Mom became sick was a dark green slipcover with gold fringe for the living room couch. So when she and Dad announced they wanted to redecorate the upstairs bedroom Sue and I shared as a special gift, I was over the moon.

The project quickly became an event. My grandmother drove up from Ohio to help us pore over wallpaper samples, paint swatches, and furniture catalogs. Mom's bed became our palette as we plopped big bulky sample books all around her, matching colors and patterns, eventually choosing wallpaper dizzy with red and pink roses. We furnished the room with all-white furniture trimmed in gold. It took several weeks, but once it was finally finished I sat on my new bed with its new sheets and matching bedspread, totally absorbed in happiness, wondering if I could have a slumber party to show it off to my friends. I felt proud — and normal.

Although she shared our excitement, Mom couldn't enjoy our decorating project as enthusiastically as we did. Too weak to go upstairs to see the bedroom transformation for herself, she had to be content with the pictures Dad took to show her what the finished room looked like.

With her illness so all-consuming, staying connected to us was a priority for Mom, so much so that she once wrote about the importance of communicating with your children for a mother-daughter banquet at our church. The banquet was an annual event, a celebration of all the women in the church, with the men volunteering to cook and serve dinner. I have vague memories of attending an earlier banquet with Mom when we first moved to Detroit, but this time she was too ill to go, so Mrs. Lang, our pastor's wife, invited Sue and me to go with her. If only by proxy, Mom was determined to have a presence there and composed the special message that she asked Mrs. Lang to read aloud during the program.

"Take time out of your too-busy day to truly look at your children and honestly listen to them," Mom wrote to the audience. "I have lots of time now to do just this and I've learned so much more about my children than ever before. Knitting and embroidery keep my hands and mind busy, but the best part of my day is when school is out and the door flies open and the kids yell, 'Mom, I'm home!' then flop on my bed with all their news of the day."

I wish I could remember the last time I flopped on her bed with news, good or bad. I wish I could remember the sound of her voice and the touch of her hand during those moments when she followed her own advice and truly looked at me. I lost those details long ago. But the lessons that resonated from all the pillow talks we shared have stayed with me throughout my adolescence and adulthood, resonating most deeply when I became a mother myself: Be present for those you love. Never give up hope. Value the time you're given.

"Despite our adversities, we still live a happy, hectic life," Mom wrote from her bed for that mother-daughter banquet, "and each day I treasure the moments I'm alive."

Mom died just months after she composed those words, five years after first discovering her cancer. Despite what our family had been through, I was caught by surprise, relentlessly clinging to my belief that she'd get well until I had no choice but to let go.

I don't think it took us long to transform the house. As I remember it, one morning I left for school and the bed was still there in its usual place, the mattress empty and stripped of linens, and when I came home that afternoon the small table and chairs from the kitchen had taken its place. The room had been dusted and vacuumed, the curtains were fresh from the dryer, and a small centerpiece sat on the table. It was back to being just as intended—The Dining Room—as if it had never had another purpose. It took us a long time to use it that way; for a full year after Mom's death, we all but ignored that table, preferring to eat our dinner on trays in front of the television in a darkened living room. Just like our house, we were in transition.

We couldn't see beyond the bed.

Let the Heart Speak

Suni Paz

The name "Ariel" sounded to me like the name of an angel. The first time I saw him, I couldn't have imagined the impact he was going to have on the thirty young students in my Spanish class at historic Erasmus Hall High School. Since 1786, this four-year public school proudly stood on Flatbush Avenue in Brooklyn, New York, and boasted of having educated famous stars like Barbara Stanwyck, Barbra Streisand, chess champion Bobby Fisher, Mae West, and opera diva Beverly Sills.

Over time, the old European-descent families moved away. By the time I started teaching, new immigrants had moved in. At a loss as to how to teach this new population of Haitians, Central Americans, Asians, Puerto Ricans, and Mexicans, the school fell academically. They desperately needed bilingual teachers, and I was hired.

I loved the atmosphere of the school with its various cultures and languages. I also cared deeply for my students who were a bit lost and trying to catch the beats of their new country and their new school. I could easily identify with them.

In 1992 Ariel entered my class. He was soft-spoken and soulful, but a hardworking and serious fourteen-year-old from El Salvador. He did all the homework I assigned on time. His appearance was delicate, and the children made fun of him because of his mannerisms. He disliked violence and was always, as the other boys said, "hiding behind the teachers' skirts." He may have been shy, but when I asked him questions about his culture, his eyes sparkled and his voice became sure and strong. He was proud of his heritage and loved to sing in his language.

In my classes, we sang a lot. I invented melodies to teach Spanish verbs and accents. We named the world with words that

Suni with students from the Spanish Club, circa 1992

came from different countries in Latin America. Thus, a kite could be called *chiringa, papalote, cometa, volantín, or barrilete.* I even wrote a song using them and the various words for string: *hilo, piolín,* and *pitilla.*

My children felt honored that I remembered their countries of origin and encouraged them to add their own indigenous vocabulary to the class word-pool. Instead of *loro*/parakeet, they would add *perico* or *brinca*/jump instead of *salta.* Ariel helped with the many Salvadorian words for food and plants that were unfamiliar to us. The students made songbooks and books about their families using photos and drawings with vivid colors. Part of the class spoke Spanish or Haitian French and the rest either an Asian language or English as a second language. Ariel was good in Spanish and became my best helper.

Mother's Day was near, and Ariel begged me if we could, *por favor,* learn and sing together some mother songs.

"Sorry, Ariel, I don't recall any."

"But, teacher, I have a tape full of mother songs. I'll lend it to you. You can learn some and then sing them with us."

He brought the tape and I felt obliged to learn at least two songs. The most beautiful was called "Madre Amor" (Mother Love):

> You carried me inside your womb and sacrificed your youth
> for me

For this and much more, I give you my gratitude.
In my darkest nights you showed me where to find light
Where my uncertainties should die and green pastures
　　come to life.
Mother love, mother love, you are the melody of my voice.
Mother love, mother love, you are my best song.

The second melody I learned for my class was a Venezuelan song by Gloria Martín, called "Cuánto Trabajo" (So Much Work). It was about a working single mother facing life's struggles and thinking only about her children. In this song, the child was the observer.

I saw her feeling alone
And as the years turned
I saw her getting old
With four children to care for

Ariel's tape reminded me that, for us in Latin America, Mother's Day was also a celebration of Mother Earth or *Pachamama*. Motherhood was respected and celebrated in song and dance. For continuity and survival, the indigenous cultures depended on procreation. They adored *Pachamama* and a woman would see in Mother Earth the qualities she wanted for herself: to be a good mother, to be dependable, grounded, nourishing, and trustworthy, and to be spiritual.

When Mother's Day arrived, every student brought something to eat. I brought my guitar and we sang the songs we'd learned and then the two mother songs. "Mother Love" was a hit. The tune was beautiful and catchy and the rhythm was contagious. We sang it over and over. Some of my students had tears in their eyes.

In a class with more boys than girls, I was surprised that they were not ashamed to show their feelings. These must have run very deep. It seemed my students were also using the song to send messages of love to their moms who were at that time either at home waiting for them or working. I wasn't sure. However, I could assume many mothers, being mostly immigrants, were at work to help provide for their family. I wondered how much contact they had with their kids.

I noticed that Ariel just cried and cried with his face buried in his arms. He didn't stop crying until the bell announced the end of the class. I asked Ariel to stay behind, as I wanted to find out what sorrow he kept hidden in his young heart.

This is what he told me:

In October 1979, struggles for power in El Salvador intensified to a civil war, disrupting city life. Political assassinations, disappearances, and bombings became daily occurrences. When the army began inducting the young, forcing them into fighting, Ariel's two older brothers escaped to the United States. Unprecedented violence menaced the lives of the people in the countryside as well. This time, fearing for Arielito, his mother dressed him as a girl and sent him out of the country hidden inside a truck. She remained in El Salvador taking care of Ariel's grandmother who was old and very ill.

In the States, the older brothers worked at night in a factory. During the day they slept, and Ariel became in charge of buying groceries, cleaning house, washing their clothes, and cooking. In turn, his brothers paid the rent and bought clothes and food for all. What a load for a youngster!

Facing me was a lonely, brokenhearted fourteen-year-old boy with heavy responsibilities, missing his mother terribly. I identified with his plight since I was also an immigrant living in the States with all my family in Argentina. And I also missed my mother. Of course, the big difference was that I could talk to her on the phone every week while Ariel had no way to communicate with his mom.

When things were not going well with my health, my work, or with my children, I would call Mother. She then would advise me.

"With your children, be softer, encourage their good side. Don't worry so much about giving your children the best of everything; just give them the best of yourself.

"In your work, don't take things in such a personal way, let things go and think positive.

"In most things, dear, follow your instincts. However, remember that at times, in life, it's necessary to put your heart in the pocket, *hay que poner el corazón en el bolsillo,* and be guided by common sense." My mother was my dearest friend on earth, my true healer.

Who did Ariel have to help him sort out from light to serious issues? Who to tell him he was loved and appreciated? Who to talk to him and heal the wounds? No one. I consulted my mom about Ariel. She was practical: "Put yourself in his shoes, then you'll know what to do . . . ."

Ariel needed a family and some friends his age. My first step was to ask him some questions about himself. Ariel's soul was still a mystery to me. My classroom was a good place to begin gathering friends, but what could be the glue that would bring Ariel and all the students in my class together in a friendly, positive way? I followed my mother's suggestion and quickly made several decisions. Then, I made him a pledge.

"You miss your mom, don't you, Ariel? Well, from now on count on me. I will be your mom in this country. Tell me anything that is in your heart and don't worry. I'm here to help you anytime. I'll find a way for you to have some good friends that will be like family to you. I promise!"

The next day, I asked my principal and the head of the language department to allow me to create a Spanish club to meet after school. The idea was joyfully approved. Most children went home to empty houses. The parents worked hard to improve their lives. The club was going to keep the students occupied until the parents were back home. It would also help keep the children away from the perils of dangerous friends, drugs, and the streets. We would practice Spanish and they would still have enough time to do their homework and complete their chores at home.

I recruited my friend, Alan, a guitar-playing teacher and expert on rock and roll songs, and a young female teacher, Sophie, with a good voice and a desire to sing. The music was varied, from folk songs to popular songs in Spanish and rock and roll in English. Now we needed some food. My children were hungry.

Ariel, who besides being a good cook was a peaceful leader, took charge of getting some parents and teachers to help with food for our meetings. He made suggestions and moms began sending Salvadorian, Mexican, and Creole goodies for our gatherings. As the club expanded, the mothers of some of our students visited us to give *consejos* or *conseils*, that is, advice on how to best keep their homes clean, cook good folk dishes, and keep away from bad company. We all relished this advice coming from their wisdom. The students listened quietly. The one whose mother was the speaker beamed with pride.

After a few months, word went around the school about our gatherings and members of the Haitian Club joined us. To our Spanish and English songs and to our pool of Caribbean dances we added some Haitian songs and dances. We kept expanding.

Some days, as we prepared the classroom for our meetings, I had conversations with Ariel about his future.

"What is your biggest dream, Ariel?"

"To be able to make a living on my own, become useful, and visit my mom in El Salvador."

"I assure you, that if you keep up your good work and graduate, jobs are going to come to you. Then all else will follow. Believe me."

"Well, now I have good friends, *maestra*, and my peers are a kind of family. I no longer feel lonely. Now I have clear goals. I think I know where I'm going."

"That's right. And you will have everything else your heart dreams of . . . you'll see."

In time, I would learn that the friendships the children made in Spanish Club lasted a lifetime. Joyous surprises came out of the club, the substance of stories I promised myself to write later.

As a docent and mother figure, I was teaching them how to work with one another, how to be loving and compassionate, to help and reassure instead of mock the weaknesses each of us showed, and above all to open their hearts and listen to one another. These were the values I learned from my mother at home and over the phone. Now I was passing them on to my students and I could already see positive results. I felt reassured.

The joy and camaraderie we shared in the club strengthened us and kept us alive and hopeful. My students were learning to share among themselves and with the visiting mothers. They went home with a handful of ideas and plenty of advice for living. They exchanged recipes and a book of recipes appeared as if by magic: *Recetas del Club de Español.*

The students no longer mocked Ariel's mannerisms, but helped him make phone calls, gather food, create lists of songs, prepare shows, and keep accounts of the little money we managed to gather for the club. Other students helped some of their peers with their homework by explaining whatever was not understood. I could see budding teachers among them.

To see them grow and share was my delight. To me, these social gatherings were living proof that poetry, music, and the content of its lyrics can positively transform young hearts. With support, I believed the youngsters would become more self-assured. They might even gather enough courage to follow a career and help change the world.

Three years later, Ariel and the other children graduated from Erasmus Hall High School. Ariel was now a confident young man, with a smiley countenance, ready to face life. Containing my tears, I saw my students leave. I was proud of their accomplishments, but I also was afraid. Would they make it? Were they prepared enough? Would life be kind to them?

A year after graduation, I found out that Ariel had become a salesman and the manager of a clothing store. I made plans to visit him.

I entered the store and saw him; we hugged.

"Ariel, you look great. How are you doing? It's so nice to see you!"

I was facing a tall, lean, and dreamy-looking young man wrapped in a tunic. His honey mane reminded me of a lion cub. His eyes sparkled.

He introduced me to his boss and clarified: "She was like a mom to me."

The owner shook my hand repeatedly saying, "So, you are his teacher! Well, I'm pleased to meet you! He always talks about you. You should then know he is my most trusted employee. He is dependable and very good at what he does."

"Yes, I know. Ariel was our most trusted person in the Spanish Club."

"He has worked very hard. I'm giving him a long vacation, so that he can visit his mom in El Salvador."

"I already bought the plane ticket, *maestra*. I'm leaving in two days."

Visit his Mom? Ariel's most desired dream was coming true. He made it happen, I thought. We embraced in farewell.

My Spanish Club colleagues, Alan and Sophie, and I had only pointed the way; the students had traced their own roads toward the future. We expected the best from our students, and because they felt our trust, love, and respect for them, they gave the most of themselves. This experience led me to the conclusion that we don't have to conceive a child in order to be a mother. But we must desire it and let our hearts speak.

Journey With Mother

Sara Etgen-Baker

The stately, timeworn building located at 400 Houston Street was like a magnificent Samuel Goldwyn movie set. I lingered at the front door with my mother and brother and imagined that perhaps Leo G. Carroll, Helen Hayes, or Sir Laurence Olivier would exit from the set onto the street where we stood.

As I stood in front of it for the first time in 1959, Union Station hypnotized me with its 1916 Beaux-Arts architecture—elegant cartouches, balustrades, pilasters, arched windows, and pediment doors. Its style made it like an aristocratic and elegant lady who'd withstood the ravages of time and appeared unchanged but oddly juxtaposed against the burgeoning, streamlined Dallas skyline. Union Station was a venerable and steadfast fixture of the downtown landscape, but the future was quietly encroaching on its almost sacred ground. It appeared Janus-faced on that warm July morning and spoke to my soul.

When I entered the building with my mother and brother, I stepped into the upper level concourse and gasped for breath—engulfed by the 48-foot vaulted ceilings. I tightly closed my eyes as I breathed in a musty, old-building smell that reminded me of my grandmother's attic. I gently touched the worn surfaces of unassuming, antiquated chairs; then I quietly waited on stiff, uncomfortable wooden benches.

While the three of us waited for our train, I sat next to my mother—entranced—as I silently watched the men, women, and children as they rushed through the lobby. The pristinely groomed men donned felt hats and wore look-alike gray flannel suits with ties, identical to the outfits Ward Cleaver wore on the *Leave it to Beaver* television show. Although not as slender, Mother reminded

me of his wife, June Cleaver—
the iconic *good American wife and
mother.*

Mother's hair was curled
and waved in a similar fashion; her dress and accessories
looked as if they came directly
from June Cleaver's closet—a
fitted-bodice dress with a circle
skirt, stockings, and pearls. She
bore the same gentle, almost ef-
fervescent smile as June Cleaver.
My mother's patience and interaction with her husband and

*Winifred Christine Stainbrook-
Etgen, circa 1947, age 20*

children compared to the relationship June had with her husband Ward, and their children, Wally and the Beaver. Mother,
like other women during this time period, conformed to the June
Cleaver image because she wanted to be the good American
mother. Conformity, the by-product of the massive conservatism,
became the mantra of the decade and was easily identifiable by
clothing choices.

Mother dressed both my brother and me in the children's at-
tire of the day: he wore a polo shirt, crisply starched khaki pants,
and sneakers, while I wore a neatly-pressed frilly dress, lace pet-
ticoat, and saddle oxford shoes—much like the characters in my
favorite school book, *Fun with Dick and Jane.*

I recall that Mother's face often reflected the 1950s enthusiasm
and optimism, as did so many others of that era. However, their
illusory euphoria—shielded in convention—was as fragile as thin
ice on an early springtime pond. Below the surface of this frail,
fallacious cultural climate, mounting fears and circumspection
about desegregation, the Cold War, nuclear war, Communism,
and McCarthyism slowly melted away the euphoric, innocentlike
atmosphere that my mother and so many Americans cherished.

Soon I heard the bigger-than-life announcement roar through
the loudspeakers: "Train 16 bound for Greenville, Texas; Durant,

Oklahoma; Atoka, Oklahoma; Muskogee, Oklahoma; and Joplin, Missouri—arriving Gate 20—train station platform below. Passengers proceed to the boarding area with your tickets."

Mother gracefully sprang into action, effortlessly corralled my brother and me close to her side, and said, "Children, hold my hands and stay close by my side as we walk down the staircase to the trains."

As the three of us hastily approached the massive staircase, my feet and legs froze in anticipation because I believed this staircase was a gigantic, enchanted portal that propelled me to all the different people and faraway places I had read about in school. Mother tugged on my arm and anxiously said, "Come on! We need to go!"

The excitement, however, was more than my small bladder could handle. "Mama, wait! I need to tinkle!" I urgently pleaded as I headed toward the first restroom I saw.

"Stop! You can't go in that restroom. Read the sign."

Glancing up, I saw the sign read *Coloreds Only.*

My mother pointed me across the hall, "*Our* restroom is here. Here's a dime; go in, and your brother and I will wait for you here. Hurry now. We don't want to miss our train!"

The sign on this restroom door read *Whites Only.* Baffled, I entered, placed the dime in the slot freeing the lock mechanism on the individual stall door, completed my task, and returned to my mother's side.

"Mama, why are there . . . ?"

"Not NOW!" she interrupted me. "NOT NOW!"

She grabbed my hand, and we clambered down to the bottom of the staircase where the train sat idling. The elusive steam from the engine was like soft, puffy cotton candy clouds that magically floated across the huge steel wheels located at my eye level. As we arrived at the steps of the train, the porter grabbed our baggage; the train's whistle blew with the urgency of my mother's whistling teakettle, then the conductor shouted, "All aboard!"

We boarded the train just in time, the conductor stamped our tickets to Springfield, Missouri, and we found seats near the train's caboose. The majestic bright red Iron Horse jolted the train forward ever so slightly and pulled my stomach up into my throat, filling me with queasy eagerness.

I forgot about the restroom incident, sat quietly, and watched the ever-changing landscape click by the windows. It was like watching an old movie without sound. I began reading *Fun with Dick and Jane*. Each time I opened the cover, the innocent water-colored world of the 1950s came to life, as did my imagination. I saw myself as Jane, for she would undoubtedly take a train trip to one of the places in my geography book. Like Jane, along the way I would make new friends and have wondrous journeys and harmless adventures with Dick, Sally, and Tim.

Our train clack-clacked through the fertile cotton and corn-fields of North Texas, and later it ground to a halt at the Katy Railroad Station in Greenville, Texas. As the train idled for pas-sengers to board, I glanced out the window, followed the engine's steam clouds as they drifted upward, and noticed a big sign hang-ing between the train station and the bus station that read: *Welcome to Greenville, Texas—Home of the Blackest Land and the Whitest People.*

Impatiently I asked, "What does that sign mean, Mama?"

My mother thought for a few seconds, then gently explained, "Well . . . because people here grow the food we eat, they're proud of their rich black soil."

"So, what does *Whitest* People mean?"

"Uh . . . " her voice trailing, ". . . the *White* folks here prefer only *White* people live in their town."

"You mean they don't like *Coloreds*?" I all but pleaded, "Why, Mama, why?"

A disapproving scowl emerged on her face. Agitated, she snarled, "SHH! Now is not the time . . . !"

I mistakenly believed I was to blame for the disappearance of my mother's otherwise patient countenance. So, I broke into uncontrollable bawling.

Mother gathered her composure, kneeled beside me, paused, and then softly said, "I need you to stop crying. I love you; I'm not angry with you at all. We'll talk about this later. Do you understand?"

Confused, I choked back the sobs and nodded in tearless compliance.

Then, respectfully, I responded, "Yes, Mama, I understand."

Although my tears subsided and I understood the need to be quiet, I simply could not grasp why all the unfamiliar sights, thoughts, and feelings seemed like arrows striking my heart. As the train left Greenville and resumed its journey through Oklahoma toward Missouri, my mother discreetly slipped me *Dick and Jane* hoping to distract me. Briefly, I returned to my sanctuary; yet the day's incidents weighed heavily on my mind.

I closed my book and thought about our colored housekeeper, Cora, whom mother hired to clean the house and to care for us. Cora was a stout, loving woman whom I sought when I hurt myself falling, became sick, or needed a baby tooth pulled. Every morning Mother and Cora shared coffee together at our kitchen table while Cora's children played with us. We even napped together. Although I knew Cora and her children's skin color was different than mine, they used the bathroom at our house. I could not understand why they were not allowed to use the same restrooms as Whites in public places. Because Cora and her children were part of our extended family, the contradiction between what I was experiencing and the reality at our home seemed illogical, hateful, deeply disturbing, and personally offensive.

I returned to my book—hoping to take some childlike solace in it. As I read, I suddenly realized, however, that my precious book contained no *Coloreds*. I quickly connected the day's events with this new realization. Without thinking, I turned to my mother and loudly said, "Mama, there are no *Colored* children in my book! How can this be?"

The bitter tears began again and streamed uncontrollably down my face. "And, why are there separate restrooms? Why? Do *Whites* not like *Coloreds*? Why?"

It was a life-altering moment for us both. My innocent, watercolored world lay shattered in pieces before my mother.

Later I realized the difficulty she faced in answering me. I imagine she wondered just how was she to guide and support me as I lifted the veil of childhood innocence. How was she to respond to my public questions in light of the cultural climate of the late fifties? How was my mother to explain the human condition, life's contradictions, and prejudicial human nature without creating prejudice in me?

Soothingly, she said, "I hadn't noticed. Let's see."

I wanted her to erase the day's incidents, erase my confusion, my fears, and somehow right my world again; so eagerly I watched her eyes as she slowly, methodically turned the pages in my book. Then, she closed the book, took my hand, and looked softly into my eyes.

Her tender and carefully orchestrated response was, "You're troubled and I understand. You're so right. There are no *Coloreds* in your book and there should be. I am grateful you are so sensitive."

Almost pleading, I again inquired, "Why aren't *Colored* children in my book?"

"I suppose the author of the book just didn't think to write the book that way."

Yet another contradiction now entered my mind. I asked, "But I thought you told me books are valuable and important. How could a book be valuable if *Coloreds* are not in it?"

"My dear sweet daughter, you've asked some adultlike questions, and you deserve answers to all of them. I will answer all your questions. Just remember, though, you will be more grown up afterward; you will understand more, but your world will never be the same. Are you ready to be more grown up?"

I looked into her soft eyes and recognized that look on her face—it was the same one I saw the day she told me the *truth about Santa Claus* as she gently nudged me out of childhood fantasy into reality. The serious tone in her voice was identical to the one she used the day she explained why she made the life-altering decision that moved me from kindergarten into first grade halfway through the school year.

I pondered and knew the direction of my life would change forever. "Yes, Mama, I am ready."

"You've just learned that sometimes people are imperfect and unkind. Imperfection is part of being human—like forgetting to hang up your clothes. The author of your book was imperfect and probably forgot to include *Colored* children in the story. Being unkind, though, is quite different. You saw unkindness today not only in the restrooms in Union Station but also on the sign in Greenville, Texas."

"What makes people unkind, Mama?"

"People are unkind for lots of reasons. Mostly, though, they are unkind because they are afraid."

"So, *Whites* are unkind to *Coloreds* because they are afraid of *Coloreds*?"

"Yes. Some *Whites* are fearful; but like you, a great many are not."

"So exactly why do *Whites* fear *Coloreds*?" I insisted.

"Sometimes people fear others who are different—regardless of the difference. The difference might be skin color, hair color, eye color, place of birth, or even religion. That fear keeps people from looking favorably at one another, seeing beyond differences, and understanding similarities. Basically, people sometimes fear what they don't understand."

I thought momentarily, then formulated my next question: "Do *Coloreds* fear *Whites*, too?"

"Yes, sweetie, fear—like kindness—is a choice people in either race can make. The fear you've seen today is called *prejudice;* it blinds people—regardless of race—to their own anger and discontent; then they often choose to react unkindly . . . remember, though, you don't have to be that way."

Then Mother reached over to me, pulled me into her arms, and hugged me. Stunned but comforted, I soon sat motionless staring out the window. The train's rhythmic clicking mesmerized me putting me to sleep.

In retrospect, Mother's wise response to my questions both soothed and changed me. Her tenderness helped me comprehend prejudice and look it squarely in the face; her calm response acknowledged the value of my sensitivity—a priceless attribute I would need as a teen and young adult in the tumultuous sixties.

Despite the surroundings and the prevailing cultural climate, my mother bravely seized that moment in order to teach me about tolerance and societal injustices; her patience, sensitivity, insight, and ability to share wisdom increased my awareness and kept me from being a mindless victim of prejudice and hate. After that journey with Mother, I saw her with new eyes; she was not like June Cleaver at all. Rather, she was both progressive and brave. Likewise, she was the quintessential mother who not only embraced courage but also modeled it for me.

Finding You Again in Bolivia, October 2010

Mariana Swann

Through the streets of La Paz your ghost follows me, Mother. I walk down the busy avenues of our capital, I visit the plazas, I raise my gaze toward the tall buildings, and I find you in every place I see.

Today I amble alone toward the center of La Paz, revisiting my past. From time to time I stop to admire the Andean mountains that encircle the capital, especially your beloved three-peaked Mount Illimani, the city's sentinel. The sky is clear, deep blue, the warm air caresses my skin, and childhood memories flood my mind.

I walk up Avenida Villazón, trying to find my primary school, Colegio Bancario, the school for the children of bank employees. There you worked as a kindergarten teacher and I spent five happy years. I believe it was here, in this short and narrow passage, grandiosely named Calle del Aviador. I enter the passage and at the end I see a two-storey, grayish-green building, a sign above the door: Instituto Bancario.

My heart beats fast. I am sure the door must be closed . . . but it is open. A few teenagers chat in groups, but there is nobody at reception. It is four o'clock; the lessons are over. The green-and-white tiled central hall, which seemed enormous when I was a girl, and where daily we sang the national anthem, has shrunk. I step into the room to my left, my old classroom, where I learned to read and write, and everything is as it was nearly fifty years ago: the long wooden planks on the floors, the old desks with names and drawings engraved deep into the wood, the dusty gray blackboards.

I leave my classroom and walk toward the preschool area, and I see you through your window smiling, surrounded by your little ones, handing out Play-Doh and colored chalk. The children sit cross-legged on the floor, their eyes on you, listening to your every word. They all want to be your favorite. I hear their giggles, their voices: "Me, me, Miss Emma! Choose me!" You pat the boys and girls on the head, sing with them, clap hands with them, and hug the ones who are feeling shy. I hear your laughter, and the room is filled with joy. I want to

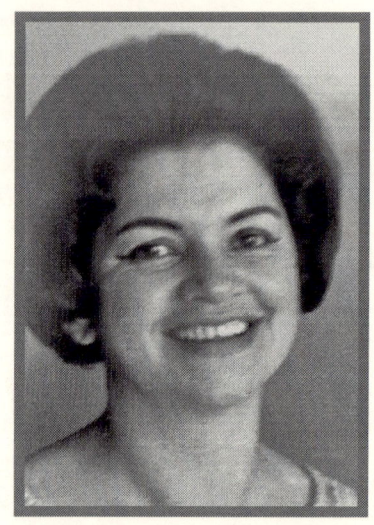

Mariana's mother, Emma Seifert, age 47, 1975

engrave this picture in my mind, but my eyes become cloudy and your image melts away like a mist.

I say good-bye to the school and continue on my way. Five minutes later, I arrive at the Student's Plaza, so called because of its proximity to Universidad Mayor de San Andrés, the main university of La Paz. I cross the street through the hellish traffic toward El Prado, one of the busiest and most elegant avenues of our city, and join the thousands of people thronging the sidewalk. Your spirit comes with me and together we enter Maria Auxiliadora Church, full of light with cream-colored walls, where we attended Mass most Sundays, and where I had my First Communion. I remember how you stayed up all night sewing the communion veils and dresses, long and white and with a blue ribbon along the border. My sister Carolina and I posed with angelic faces for the photos, looking like younger versions of Mother Teresa, after which we went back to our usual mischievous behavior.

After a short prayer, your spirit and I leave the church and continue toward the end of El Prado, where we find the proud statue of our Liberator, Simón Bolívar, sitting on his white stallion and pointing his sword toward the independence of half a continent. The cinema of the same name, where you took my sisters and me to watch so many Walt Disney films, has now become a shoe shop. I cross the street and go up toward the main square of La Paz, Plaza Murillo, to visit the Cathedral and the Museo Nacional de Arte, and you come with me, my constant companion.

I am tired and thirsty now. The sun is at its zenith; people start to leave their offices in search of lunch. At a cafeteria near Plaza Murillo I order a coffee and two savory *salteña* pastries filled with spicy chicken and diced potatoes. They are delicious, but not as good as the ones you used to make.

Your image is vivid in my mind, and my thoughts take me back to the events of the previous day. Yesterday I visited your house, Mamá, your humble house in the country where you spent your last years, and where you suffered long days of solitude, your three daughters in faraway places; but where, as the courageous and optimistic woman that you were, you shook away all negative thoughts, dusted yourself off, and got on with living.

What a comfort it is to think that at the end you were not so alone, thanks to Carolina and Teresa, my younger sisters, who came back to Bolivia to provide you with companionship and affection in your final days. I, living in another continent, tied to my British family, was only able to offer you a little of what I so much wanted to give you: love and support. When you came to see me during your last visit to England, I looked after you. Do you remember how I persuaded you to do your exercises? How I gently reprimanded you whenever you considered yourself an old woman with stiff muscles? Do you remember how I looked after your diet? How I pampered and loved you? But I noticed your frailty. All of a sudden, although your mind was as sharp as ever, you had become an old lady, unsteady on your feet, walking slowly, climbing the stairs with difficulty.

In England we spent many happy hours cooking, baking, going for walks. But mainly, we spent time talking about our lives and our hopes for the future. I wanted to know more about your past, so I interviewed you. You told me a few things, mainly happy ones, but I am aware that you kept to yourself several painful episodes, private things that neither my sisters nor I were entitled to know. I respected your privacy, as you did mine. Now that you are gone, I wish I had learned more about your life, about our common past, but I must accept that revealing certain things to me would have opened up your secret box of sorrows and regrets. Sometimes it is preferable to live in blissful ignorance—much better to remember you as the cheerful woman that you were until the very end.

We also had one or two disagreements, which made both of us unhappy. You commented upon my being too strict with my children and too impatient with my husband.

"Mamá, you don't know what it's like for me here, all alone with mountains of housework and no one to relieve me of the constant childcare!" I protested. And you replied that life was too short to squander it getting stressed. I was indeed stressed. I was going through a difficult period in my marriage and was having trouble coping with family life. I had wanted you to be fully on my side; instead you seemed to be looking at things with a cool and impartial eye. I thought you were a little harsh and unsympathetic toward me, but as the days went by, I started to think that maybe you had a point.

Before you returned to Bolivia, we decided you deserved a treat, so you came along with my family to the Canary Islands. As usual, we discussed politics, talked about our favorite books, gossiped about our acquaintances; and, again, you hinted that I was still a bit too impatient with my husband and children. This time your wise words did not upset me. On the contrary, I welcomed your advice. I knew that my happiness was important to you. I knew that what you were telling me was right. In order to have a happier family life, I needed to stop making demands on other people, and I needed to take a good look at myself instead. Thank you, Mamá, for alerting me to my defects and for encouraging me to reflect.

I often think of the hard life you had. You were a divorced woman living in a Catholic, conservative, and male-dominated society. You were also a liberated and hardworking mother who believed that, through education, a girl could achieve anything she wanted.

Yesterday I crossed the threshold of your old house in the country, in Achumani, on the outskirts of La Paz, which Teresa has kept exactly as it was the day you died. You were there, waiting for me, looking at me with your sweet big eyes from every photograph. Your ghost was hiding behind each potted plant, behind each object that I, eager to find you, touched, smelled, caressed. You were there, sitting on the stool by the little telephone table of carved dark wood, made by a master Bolivian woodcarver. You were there, like a noble Spanish *maja*, beside the chest of drawers, also of carved wood, your pride and glory, your exquisite taste. The ravages of time and the many blows that life gave you took away some of your beauty, but your spirit remained indomitable. Until the very end you maintained that everything would be all right, that soon your problems would be over . . . but it saddens me to think that your twilight years were filled with worry.

I then saw you standing in your kitchen, kneading bread on the table, wearing your long white apron and with flour up to your elbows, pounding the dough, your hair tied in a bun. There you were, making cheese *empanadas* dusted with sugar, their smell filling the house.

The ghosts of my childhood and adolescence were also waiting for me at your house: on a wall, the photo of your three princesses, wearing fluffy dresses of white tulle and red ribbons. To celebrate the coronation of the school queen on the first day of spring, the three of us would enter the school hall to the music of Verdi's *Aïda*. Three little girls made of cotton candy, smiling for you on a brilliant sunny day.

In the spare bedroom I found an old blanket. That ancient thick red blanket with two thin white stripes, one on each opposite side, reminded me of your bed with the metal frame, and I saw myself as a child, covered by that same itchy blanket, shivering during the cruel winters of La Paz and crying myself to sleep. During my childhood you worked two evenings a week at the Spanish Embassy, helping to organize that institution's cultural activities. At school I would boast to my friends that you were the Spanish ambassador! I remember the art book you brought home one day and how I immediately fell in love with one of the most beautiful paintings I had ever seen: *Las Meninas* by Diego Velázquez. On those lonely nights, I missed your warmth and your caresses. To console myself, I would hug your nightie to breathe in its faint perfume.

Three part-time jobs you had. You worked as a kindergarten teacher in the mornings, as a clerk at an insurance company in the afternoons, and as a secretary at the Spanish Embassy two evenings per week. You had to support three young daughters and our grandmamá.

I entered the bedroom that you shared with my son Christopher when we visited you in 1998. On top of the bedside table was a photograph of Christopher and my husband, Jim, in our home in England. On the windowsill, among your papers and toiletries, I discovered a photo of my daughter, Olivia, aged eight or nine, wearing a pink lacy dress, holding hands with you. Our past lives, countries, and cultures, all mixed together.

Tears pricked my eyes. I opened the doors and drawers of your wardrobe, and I found you there, too. Your clothes made a profound impact on me. I caressed, touched, and smelled your blouses; I wanted to engrave them in my mind. Your gray suit of English cloth and in English style, your pleated red skirt, your white and green shirts.

Mamá, where have your spirit, your laughter, and your joy gone? All we have left are our memories of you and of the good example you set, your photographs, a few letters. You had virtues and you had defects, but you were a good and loving mother. You taught me to think of others and to show them respect and tenderness. Thank you for everything you gave me, and for your infinite love.

And now you return to the ghostly home you have inhabited for the past seven years. But I know you will come back; I know that tomorrow you will follow me through the streets of our capital, and that I will again find you in each and every object that you touched, in the three-peaked Mount Illimani that you so loved, in the clear sky of La Paz, in our country.

In memory of my mother, Emma Seifert
(Tarija, March 1928 – La Paz, September 2003)

What More Could a Daughter Ask?

Maria Klassen

I walk down the long hall to my mother's room every Sunday afternoon. I pass Myrna, a frail-looking woman with short-cropped hair sitting in a wheelchair, head leaning forward, making eye contact with no one. Olive, who is slight and stooped, pushes her and I have no idea where she gets the strength to move the wheelchair. I greet Peter as I pass the table where he is working on a jigsaw puzzle, nose running, hands trembling, mouth drooping. He nods his head ever so slightly in acknowledgment.

I enter my mother's room, always with a sense of despair after the walk down the hall. My mother's face lights up and she greets me with a smile, a hug, and a kiss. I don't know how she can be so cheerful when she lives with disease and death, on the other side of her door, every day of her life. She really shouldn't be living here I think to myself again. But we have hashed through this many times. My father needed the assistance of a long-term care home in the small Ontario town they lived in, about half an hour's drive from where I live.

When he asked my mother to move in with him, she didn't think twice—she had married him for better or worse, and she would go with him. He died two years later, and we offered her several choices of where to live. She decided to stay; the transition had been hard for her, and she didn't want to move out just to move in again. So it was her decision to stay—I question it every visit—should I have pushed harder for her to change her mind?

Inside her room I momentarily forget what is on the other side of her door. We quickly move into another world, her world. We go on a journey, delving into her past. She has kept diaries of her life and, since I have visited Neuendorf, the village in the

Ukraine where she spent her first twenty years, I can picture the places she remembers. Every Sunday afternoon I add a bit more to my history.

She often has music playing when I come into her room. If her knees weren't crippled with arthritis, I swear she would be dancing. On Saturday afternoons (when I was growing up), when the house was tidy and the chores were done, she would put on music and we would dance around the dining room table. I still love a Strauss waltz.

Maria's Mother, 89 years young

I look at her closely. She is wearing a soft pink sweater that complements her gray hair. She always wears her strand of pearls, given to her by my father on their twenty-fifth wedding anniversary, when his business was doing well. She does not look eighty-nine years old. She has aged gracefully. I can only hope I have inherited her genes. She has wrinkles, but fewer than women twenty years younger. Her face does not reflect the hard years of her life.

She always asks about my children, her grandchildren. Family is so important to her since she had sixteen siblings. She has told me many times how often her mother was pregnant. That is one of the pictures she has of her mother—always pregnant. Only nine children lived to become adults. She tells of a sister who died in Poland, a country they lived in briefly as they were fleeing from one country to another from the Ukrainian village to the refugee camp in Germany, during WWII. She tells of another sister who was born in Poland on the trek from the Ukraine to Germany. This sister survived.

She tells of twin brothers who were born prematurely in Neuendorf and died within two days, as there was no hospital, clinic, doctor, or nurse who knew what to do in the village of the communist country where they lived. Her mother nearly lost her life giving birth and was unable to care for the twins. Her father set them on clean straw by the wood stove to keep them warm, but it was not enough.

My mother was too young to help or even know what was happening. The weak cries of death haunted her for years. Does one ever become immune to the ravages of death? My mother's mother lost her parents as a teenager. They died within days of each other. A few years before that, my grandmother's three siblings died within hours of each other and their funerals were on the same day. When the family came home from the funeral, a fourth sibling had died. All from the deadly disease of typhus fever that spread through the Mennonite villages. My mother thought of her mother as a heroine—because she had faced death so many times and was able to go on living in spite of the tremendous pain.

We speak German. My mother grew up speaking a Dutch dialect similar to German that the Mennonites had brought with them when they migrated from the land around the Dutch-German border over a hundred years previously. It wasn't a written language. So with her children she spoke German, a proper language that we could read and write. I have little opportunity to speak it, so I appreciate keeping up my language skills in conversations with her.

Then she asks me how I am doing. This is also important to her as she nursed me through years of a life-threatening illness. I will never forget how encouraging she was. She would cook anything I wanted just so I would eat. She supplied me with books of various genres; we still share a love for reading and read some of the same books. She always had an amusing story to tell me then: what was happening in the neighborhood, or something she had read, or an original tale. I never saw her discouraged with my health issues or me. Many years later, she shared her worries and concerns, her personal battle with the possibility of losing me, her first-born child; but I never saw that—ever.

In keeping with our routine, the next topic is our country. She has always loved Canada, from the moment she set her foot on its soil to this very day. It means freedom for her—freedom of speech, freedom of religion, freedom of choice, and free will, and so much more. I know the story of how she had to quit school at age thirteen to work at the local store to help support her family. When the school officials came to ask her why she wasn't in school, she had to lie and say she didn't like school and didn't want to go anymore. If she had told the truth, her father would have gone to a labor camp in the far north, never to be seen again; it had happened to other men in the village. She was fiercely determined to protect her family. She loved them all so very much. That is all they had in those years after the Revolution, during the famine years, and then during WWII—each other.

Next she asks me if I was in church. I hear her voice in my head every Sunday morning, and sometimes I go, just to get that voice out of my head. God and faith sustained her through many hard years, when she didn't know if, or how, she and her family would survive. This, she says, is the most important part of your life, your faith in God. She grew up without being able to attend church. During the communist era all the churches were closed down or converted for other uses. Parents were not allowed to talk to their children about God or read the Bible in their own homes.

At state-run schools, innocent young children were asked what their parents talked about. If religion was mentioned, a wrong answer, a one-way ticket was given to that parent to the labor camps in the north, to Siberia. Parents couldn't take the chance of a little one being tripped up; so religious training was done when the children were older, in secret. Probably because of this restraint during her formative years, she appreciates any religious and spiritual food that she can glean. She appreciates the fact that she can talk about religion as often as she wants, with whomever she wants.

We then share a treat I have brought. She so loved cooking and baking and made many ethnic dishes for us—borscht, vareniki, perishki, pfefferminz and kuchen, and zwieback. Now I try to bring her a taste of some of those special ethnic dishes, like platz or paska. She is always so appreciative of anything I bring. She vividly remembers the many years of famine she and her family experienced in the Ukraine. She tells me stories of how she admired her mother for making meals and feeding all her children with no ingredients, using bark to make a "soup" or making a loaf of black bread stretch for days. When my mother sees how food is thrown away in our society, she feels such waste is the ultimate sin.

There were times in her childhood that the only way the family survived was because of care packages sent to them from relatives already in Canada. When she arrived in Canada and her family was able to join her, she loved to have them over for a meal. She enjoyed having people in her home, and I remember always having company, sometimes for a meal, sometimes overnight, and sometimes for many nights. She often invited people who didn't have family to our house, especially for special celebrations like Christmas. She didn't want anyone to be alone on the holidays.

My mother loved to have the extended family gather at our house on weekends. I grew up with many cousins and still see many of them regularly. It didn't matter who or how many people dropped in on a Sunday afternoon, there was always, and I mean always, enough food for everyone. And the laughter, never did I hear an argument, always good clean fun. My uncles could entertain us children with a simple toy for hours. She still sees her surviving siblings on a regular basis; they celebrate all birthdays.

I have observed how she deals with the other residents in the home. She sits with someone who isn't mobile, pushes a wheelchair for someone who wants to go somewhere. She butters the bread of one of her tablemates. She holds the songbook for someone who can't. She brings in jigsaw puzzles and lends many of her books to others, knowing she may never get them back. She is patient. She listens. She seldom complains and is always appreciative of what she has. And my life lessons continue . . . .

So I spend my Sunday afternoons with my mother, because I think Sunday afternoons should be spent with family. We talk and we laugh; we cry and we eat. I stand in awe of a woman who came from so little and learned to give so much. She modeled commitment, affection, optimism, style, realism, family, health, patriotism, faith, culture, history, appreciation of good food, compassion, the love for language and music. She knew that attitude and gratitude were important, long before they became fashionable buzzwords. She is my definition of love. She gave me roots, and she gave me wings. She taught me, and still teaches me, by her life.

What more could a daughter ask?

Puo-puo

Angela Tung

*E*ach time I talk to my mother she sounds like she's been crying.

"The funeral is Thursday," she tells me. "Dad and I are flying to L.A. on Tuesday, and will stay with Big Uncle. You and Alex come down on Wednesday."

"Okay," I say. Alex, my boyfriend, and I live in San Francisco, and my brother, Greg, has plenty of space to put us up. My parents are the ones with the long flight from New Jersey. "How are you doing, Mom?" I ask. It's her mother who has died.

"Okay," she says, her voice crumbling. Then she finishes quickly, "We'll call when we land." She hangs up.

We all knew my grandmother didn't have much time. Puo-puo was ninety-four. She had a calcified knee that gave her great pain and limited mobility, but she refused surgery, as she was afraid of going under the anesthesia and never waking up. In the last few years, she had a series of small strokes, which left her increasingly debilitated until she could no longer speak.

The last time I saw her, just a couple of months before the funeral, I barely recognized her. Gone was the plump and lively grandmother who rolled delicious dumplings, kicked everyone's butts at mah-jongg, and once ripped out barehanded, a barely-loose tooth from my seven-year-old jaw. Instead, an emaciated old lady stared blankly at me from her bed.

"It's Little Gem!" I told her, calling myself by the Chinese nickname my grandfather had given me. "It's Little Gem!" She didn't answer.

But her death is still a shock. One moment she was in the hospital for a fever, the next she was gone.

My first memory of Puo-puo was when I was four. Greg had just been born, and Puo-puo had come from California to help my mother. While she was busy with my brother, Puo-puo fed me boiled eggs in rice porridge and listened to me chatter. I picked up her Shandong accent.

After Greg grew bigger, Puo-puo visited just once a year. When she did, she always made delicious dumplings, pot stickers, and *mantou*, the soft

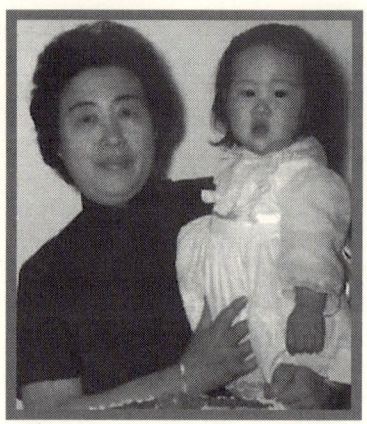

Puo-puo at Angela's first birthday

steamed bread. She took the extra dough and molded us doves with delicate wings and sharp beaks. She tolerated my silly jokes, like the time I put a fake mouse in her purse. She screamed, but then burst out laughing.

Unlike my mother, Puo-puo never yelled at me, not even the time I peed my pants and tried to hide them in a drawer. Or when I dropped a glob of minced pork on the floor when she was trying to teach me how to make dumplings. My mother, a phenomenal cook but an impatient teacher, never taught me. It was easier if we stayed out of her way.

Mom, like all my aunts and uncles, cared what Puo-puo thought. She cared about how we behaved around her and our grandfather, especially when we became sullen and surly teenagers. Were we polite enough? Did we greet them in the morning and in Chinese? "Gong-gong *zhao*, Puo-puo *zhao*." Was I thin enough? Or would Puo-puo make comments about my weight the way she had about my mother's when she was a girl, the way she did about everybody's?

"Can you lose five pounds in one week?" my mother would ask me before my grandparents' visit.

At the most I was chubby, but to my mother and Puo-puo, I might as well have been obese. I didn't know how to keep my weight consistent. Sometimes I was effortlessly trim; other times I bulged in the wrong places. I'd diet stupidly, eating nothing all day, then gorging myself when I got home from school.

"You look so sloppy," my mother would say, hoping her harsh words would encourage me to slim down. "You walk so heavy. Your legs are so thick."

I wanted to be skinny, like the girls in the magazines. I wanted my mother to compliment me, the way she did when I got A's or did well with piano. But at the same time, I resented her constant criticism.

Once when Puo-puo was visiting, I refused to eat for a day. We went out to lunch at the mall, and I ordered nothing. If Mom thought I was fat, I told myself, then I'd starve.

"You're eating nothing?" Puo-puo asked. Although I needed to lose weight, she thought, I still had to eat something. "Nothing at all?"

I crossed my arms. "I'm not hungry," I said.

"Have some soup," my mother said. "Or a salad."

"I'm not hungry."

I was fourteen. The only power I had over my mother was my refusal.

"How can she eat nothing?" Puo-puo went on. "She can't eat nothing."

Mom got teary then. In her mother's eyes, she was failing. She was the daughter who'd never be good enough.

My brother picks us up at the airport. It's past midnight, and we're exhausted, but at least there's no traffic. The night before, Greg had picked up our parents and slogged through rush hour to bring them to Big Uncle's house in Orange County.

He asks, "Why did Mom want us to drive seven hours to Palo Alto?"

I shake my head. While the funeral is in L.A., the burial is in Palo Alto, where Gong-gong is buried. For two decades, my grandparents lived in nearby Berkeley. Puo-puo only moved in with Big Uncle, her elder son, after Gong-gong died.

"Who knows?" I say. "She thought it was more trouble getting to and from the airport. But then she heard Big Uncle was flying, so we're flying now, too."

Greg sighs.

The night before, in the car, our mother seemed fine, Greg will tell me later. But then they arrived at Big Uncle's house, and the moment she saw her younger brother, she burst into tears. Big Uncle cried the whole time. He tried to tell them what happened: Puo-puo's fever, the days in the hospital, how they sent her home and she died the very next day. How he thought if he had fought for her to stay at the hospital, she might have lived. How the care-taker woke him early the next morning to tell him, "Something is wrong with Mrs. Lee!" and he ran over, heart pounding, and tried to give her CPR. How he had tried to save her one last time.

For now I don't know this. We shake our heads at our moth-er's nuttiness, her confused planning. I think of the speech I have to make, along with some of the other grandchildren, the next day. I try not to be nervous. Although it's not about me, I want to do well. I want my mother to be proud of me.

When I was in college, my parents tried to convince me to go to law school. "Lots of English majors become lawyers," they told me, as though this somehow was incentive.

It wasn't. I wanted to be a writer, and that was that.

I applied to writing schools.

"We'll pay for it," my father said, but I declined.

I'd go to a city school, take out loans, keep working and go to school part-time— anything to avoid my mother's resentment at having to pay for something she didn't approve.

In the end I got a full scholarship to a program in Boston. I was living at home then and yelled the news to my mother through the bathroom door as she finished her shower.

"Whoo!" she whooped over and over. "Whoo!"

By then I was dating the man who'd become my husband, though my mother didn't know. She disapproved of him for rea-sons she couldn't express. I know now it was because she could sense his dislike for her, his thinking his family was better than ours, that I was lucky to have him.

But even if my mother had told me these things, I wouldn't have believed her. I wouldn't realize she was right until much later. Until after my husband had an affair and impregnated his mistress, until our divorce. I wouldn't believe her until I met Alex, who considered himself the lucky one and was kind to my mother out of kindness to me.

At the funeral my mother never removes her sunglasses.

The moment we arrive, she grabs my brother and me and leads us over to Puo-puo's coffin. I'm almost surprised by the tiny elderly woman with the snowy coif. That's not Puo-puo, I keep thinking as we bow once, twice, three times. Puo-puo has a jet-black perm. Puo-puo has cheeks as plush as *mantou*. Puo-puo laughs so hard her eyes squeeze shut as though she can hardly contain herself.

In the pew behind my parents, I turn my speech over and over in my hands. I'm getting more anxious; I feel selfish about being anxious.

We sit. The choir sings "Amazing Grace." Finally, my uncle Wen Ray, the youngest of the five siblings, goes up to the dais and tells the stories everyone knows.

My grandmother was born in 1918 in Weihai, a tiny seaside village in Shandong province. When she was eighteen, she married Gong-gong, the youngest son of the richest family in town. During World War II, he was imprisoned by the Japanese. Puo-puo went to the jail to demand to know what was going on. Just a few years later, at the onset of the Communist Revolution, Gong-gong was captured again. He was made to wear a dunce cap with the characters Traitor, Counter-Revolutionary, Bourgeoisie. Shortly after his release, he escaped to his sister's in Qingdao. The Communists came pounding on Puo-puo's door looking for him.

"I don't know where he is!" she cried. "He just left us!"

Months later, she followed him. It was a long, hot wagon ride with my elder aunt, my mother, and Big Uncle, just a toddler then. During their year in hiding they bore another child, my aunt Ping, before finally boarding a boat to Taiwan, where their last child, Wen Ray, was born. When their children grew up, one by one they left

Taiwan for graduate school in the United States, bringing Gong-gong and Puo-puo over to Berkeley in 1972, the year I was born.

When my uncle finishes, he's crying. Then, one after another, my cousins speak.

Todd tells the story that despite her bad knee, Puo-puo would disappear like a specter when he'd take her grocery shopping, no matter how many times he asked her to wait while he parked the car. Albert, the eldest, talks about how Puo-puo taught him mah-jongg and would stand over his shoulder berating his every move, until finally she'd say, "Okay, take a break, I'll play for you now." Justine, the youngest, says, "I told my grandmother everything; I told her things I didn't even tell my parents."

Everyone mentions Puo-puo's delectable dumplings, pot stickers, and scallion pancakes, which she sold out of her Berkeley house for twenty-five cents each. People came from all over the Bay Area to buy them, and with that dumpling money she was able to pay off the mortgage on that house and put a down payment on another. Even after Gong-gong died, she was so reluctant to leave her house, as she loved having a place big enough for all her family to visit.

Nothing scared Puo-puo, not the Japanese or the Communists. Not crossing the ocean on a boat or a plane. Not living in a country where she didn't know the language, or starting a business to fulfill her dream. All she was afraid of was being alone, and, like all of us, of dying, which perhaps is the same thing.

Then it's my turn.

Like my cousins, I tell funny, loving stories. How Puo-puo was a terrible karaoke singer. How she taught me Chinese during the summers and tested me like a real teacher. How at all-you-can-eat-buffet, she'd grimace and mutter, "Doesn't taste good," all the while eating everything off her plate, then going up for seconds. How she yanked out my reluctant tooth.

"While Puo-puo could be tough," I say, "I know she did everything out of love."

At that moment, I realize I'm not only talking about Puo-puo. I glance at my mother, her eyes still hidden. I remember how pained she and my father were upon learning of my husband's affair, how they chided me for waiting a whole year to leave, for not telling them right away. I thought they were accusing me of mistakes.

"I wish you didn't have to go through all that," my mother had said, her voice breaking.

"With Puo-puo," I continued, "I always felt loved. I always knew she thought I was precious." I stop and swallow. "That I deserved the best. I hope she knows that we all feel the same way about her."

As I return to my seat, my father reaches out and squeezes my hand. Alex puts his arms around me.

My mother's neck is bent. She can't look at me, I know. It's too difficult. But part of me still wonders if she liked my speech. Part of me would like to hear her say I did well.

Afterward, in the parking lot, we take a long time saying good-bye. We're all seeing each other again the next day for the burial, but it feels like something is over. We've all said good-bye and won't see Puo-puo again.

My mother hugs Big Uncle. "You did a good job," she tells him, her voice shaking, almost breaking but not quite, and I know she means more than just the funeral. She means he's done a good job all these years caring for Puo-puo and that he's been a good son—there was nothing more he could have done to save her.

And I realize it's my uncle who needs to hear these words, not me, not any of the cousins. He needs to hear them from my mother, his older sister, usually so hard with her words.

That night, I dream of Puo-puo. I'm in a room and I'm waiting for her, not with dread but eager anticipation. She hurries in. She's as I remember her—walking and smiling broadly, her lips bright with lipstick. She walks fast toward me and beams the way she did upon seeing any of her grandchildren.

"My knee is fixed!" she tells me. She saunters back and forth, showing off. "See?"

"I see, Puo-puo," I say, and I can't wait to tell my mother. I know she will be happy.

Endearing Gift

Barbara Kitscher

My mother, Hattie, married Tony in June 1930 in the small rural town of Petoskey in Michigan's Lower Peninsula during the time of the Great Depression.

Less than a year later, Hattie underwent major surgery that according to the medical profession should render her childless. During the course of the surgery, the doctor came out to talk to Tony. "I'll do what I can, but I need to tell you that it will be a miracle if she ever conceives a child," he said.

Saddened at the prospects of never having a child of her own, but happy to be alive and gaining strength physically, Hattie knew there were more immediate needs pressing. She and Tony were now broke after paying back the hundred dollars they borrowed from Old Charlie to get married plus the money they paid out for Hattie's surgery.

Times had not improved, and work was still hard to find. Together they planted a garden in the backyard of the one-room house where they lived in exchange for work. They canned everything they could grow or pick in the wild. Hattie even canned dandelion greens as well as the rabbits Tony shot in order to make it through the coming winter. Tony, for his part, took any work he could find. At one time, he worked for a nickel a day plus a meal.

Although they continued to struggle, their dream of having children never died. They even spoke of adopting when their plight improved, for Hattie could not accept that she was to journey through life childless. Hattie lived during a time when having twelve or more children was the norm. She and Tony had both come from large families and longed for the same blessing in their lives.

After praying for children, although she had been told that it would be a miracle if she ever conceived, Hattie was ecstatic when she found herself pregnant three years after she and Tony were married. After nine long months of waiting, a girl child was born and they named her Gertrude.

Even though they were delighted with this gift daughter, they tried, hoped, and prayed for more children. But it would be nine long years before they

Barbara's mother with Lawrence, 1949

were blessed with another. This time a son was born. Hattie nurtured this gift of life, but worried about him. He cried, failed to grow, and seemed in pain most of the time. Discovering his intolerance to cow's milk, they purchased a goat and he began to thrive and grow.

From then on the blessings continued and Tony and Hattie were now up to miracle number six. The years 1933, 1942, 1943, 1946, 1947 and 1949 were years of miracles. I was the miracle born in 1946. Could the doctor have made a mistake all those many years ago? Nothing is impossible with God for His ways are not our ways.

Hattie watched over us and kept track of each child like a mother lion to her cubs. She had a built-in sixth sense and was keenly aware of each child and his whereabouts at all times. You might say she gave new meaning to the saying "eyes in the back of the head." The story about one of her greatest challenges as a young mother is one I'll never forget.

It was a warm summer morning in 1949; Hattie was making bread while four of her young children played outside. When she heard the rattle of a large metal spoon against a barrel, she tore out of the house to investigate. The moment she saw the open well-house door, she knew without a doubt that Barbara (that's me) had been playing with a spoon and must have found her way in to the gas barrel. Since Norbert and I were only fourteen months apart, Mother also knew that wherever I was, Norbert was sure to be there, too.

As she rounded the corner, there was her two-year-old on the ground with me hovering over him. Smelling gas, Mother scooped him up and shook him to no avail and then she ran toward the highway to flag down a car. Halfway there she turned around, knowing it was no use. There just wasn't time. Even if Tony had not been at work and the car had been in the driveway, it would have made no difference.

She ran back to the sidewalk, yelling for Gertrude to bring milk, all the while willing her precious bundle to breathe. As she stood on the sidewalk outside the house, watching the life ebb from her dear child, Gertrude arrived to find out what Mother wanted. Mother yelled again, "Get some milk!"

Sizing up the situation, Gertrude raced back into the house. At the same time, my six-year-old sister, Margaret, and my seven-year-old brother, Leonard, were jumping up and down on the sidewalk yelling, "Mama, don't let him die." Sensing my mother's helplessness and seeing the panic on her face and that of my sisters and brother, I too began jumping up and down, shaking my arms and yelling, "Mama, Mama, don't let him die."

When my sister arrived with the milk, mother had to pry open her precious toddler's mouth, as he was definitely closer to death than life. His eyes were rolling back in his head and he was going limp. While my big sister poured in some milk, Leonard, Margaret, and I continued to scream.

As the milk cut the gas fumes, my brother took a breath that was more like a gasp. Then he began to cry, a frightened piercing cry. As Mother hugged him to her, she too broke down and cried, but her tears were tears of relief and joy for this child that she almost lost.

When the immediate crisis was over, Mother, with Norbert in her arms, for she wasn't about to put him down, went in the house to call the doctor. The doctor said he didn't believe there was any immediate need to see the child. He did suggest a little Coke might be a good tonic for it would allow the little tyke to burp up any lasting fumes.

The scenes of this day are forever etched in my mind's eye as my earliest memory. Even today, I can close my eyes and see and hear the events of that terrifying day unfold as if it were yesterday.

Never again was the well-house door left open where inquisitive children, like me, could get inside at the barrel that housed the gas for the tractor. Apparently, I had managed to get some gasoline on my spoon and offered it to my brother. I had seen my mother taste the food off the end of a spoon to see if it was seasoned correctly or spoon food into my little brother's mouth as he sat in the high chair. I was only imitating what I had seen my mother do.

Even though I was only three years old, I learned how very precious and loved each child was to my mother. As time went on, the lesson only grew and became a deeper part of me. It wasn't so much what my mother said, but what she did. Actions really do speak louder than words.

Over the years, I've observed how she treated each person who came into her life. Her example of love and care for others was her most endearing gift to me, second only to the very life she gave me.

At the age of five or six, while I was playing in the yard one summer day with my brothers and sisters, an older bearded man—who I later learned was probably a tramp—ventured into our yard with his little white dog. My older brother ran ahead to tell Mother. The rest of us children followed the man and his dog to the house.

The man explained that the life he was living was not a good life for his beloved dog. He said he had seen the children playing in the yard and knew without a doubt that this would be a good home for his dog. Mother without hesitation fed the man and agreed to give the dog a home. The man thanked her and, after eating, hugged his dog and told her to stay, and then he turned to resume his wandering.

Mother's own parents were loved and revered until the day they died. But not only by her, for she taught her children to do the same. Spending time with them, playing cards, or going fishing on the river was always seen as a privilege and never as a burden.

When her parents could no longer live by themselves, they prepared to sell their home and live in a house built by us. In fact, the foundation was already dug. Then they changed their minds and bought a trailer instead, which was placed at the edge of our lawn next to our woods.

Valued by our family, they were now far enough away to maintain their independence, but close enough for help if needed. Mother even had a phone line set up between the trailer and our house in case they needed help in the middle of the night.

Mother never tired of reaching out in love. When I was around ten years old, my cousin and his wife had their first child, but for some reason the baby was released from the hospital before the mother. My cousin didn't know what to do. How was he to care for his newborn infant and work too? It was my mother who came to their rescue and offered to bring the baby into our home and care for him for several days until mother, father, and baby could be reunited.

Later, when I was in eighth grade, my grandmother went into the hospital, but sadly never came home. After she passed away, my grandfather moved into our home. Living closely with my grandfather, I had a better understanding about where my mother got her warmth and great respect for life. She had had a good role model in my grandfather, for he was a deep, warm, caring individual. I knew he loved us by his actions. He played games with us, helped us do our chores, and even let my little brothers climb on him whenever he sat down. To this day, I can picture him with his arms around them, one child on his lap and two perched on either arm of his chair.

When her seven children grew up and married, Mother now had an extended family to love and cherish. Over the years she looked for any excuse to have a party to bring us all together. With the birth of each grandchild and great-grandchild, she was as elated as if each were her own. In some respect they were her own, for she had begun this legacy of life.

In her late eighties, after living a long life, mother began to show signs of dementia. Then in her early nineties, when she was in the full grip of the dreadful mind-robbing disease known as Alzheimer's and her needs were beyond our ability, she spent her remaining days in a facility with a wing equipped for the care of such patients. At times, her brain would make connections and she would light up in recognition when we came to visit. More times than not, though, the connection was lacking and the light could not be turned on.

On one visit, after mother had been in this facility for a number of months, a nurse approached me and asked me about an observation several nurses and aides alike had made.

Her question to me was this, "Did your mother ever lose a child?"

"No, why do you ask?"

"Well, several of us have noticed that your mother's face lights up and she reaches out to children when they come to visit. She also likes holding baby dolls."

"Oh, I can explain that to you. You see Mother had seven children, but she wasn't supposed to have any according to the medical profession. When she did have children, four boys and three girls, all of us were seen and watched over as precious gifts from God. I believe that her respect for life and love for humanity were such a deep part of her that these gifts never left her even when her brain no longer cooperated."

Life Is What You Make It Be

Linda Sievers

*I*t was July 1955 in Springfield, Illinois, beloved hometown of inspired political speaker, humorist, and sixteenth president of the United States, Abraham Lincoln. The air was sultry and still. Laundry my grandma had pinned that morning to the clothesline stretching across our back yard hung shapeless in the sweltering heat. No birds pecked amidst the grass in search of bugs, but rather remained hidden high among the maple and elm branches. No breezes rustled the delicate pink peony blossoms along the picket fence. Only the persistent buzz of an occasional bee penetrated the humidity.

Across the street at the Miller's house, a black canvas baby buggy sat empty on the lawn. Evidence of eight children ages eleven and under was visible by the abandoned disarray of scooter, baseball mitt, and tricycles and bicycles splayed across the yard and driveway. A single basketball gleamed in the sun. Next door, Mrs. Armin's 1935 Sears Roebuck house, partially shaded by a large oak, stood silent and dark behind closed venetian blinds. Soon, neighborhood fathers would drive lazily home from the Sangamo Electric Plant; their car windows open in an attempt to circulate air inside their vehicles. It took courage to open the car door and feel an oven-hot blast before sliding onto searing vinyl seats. It almost made the tedium of assembly lines inside an air-conditioned factory preferable.

My family did not have air conditioning. We had large fans. One stood in our dining room on top of my grandmother's tall old china cabinet. Another rattled in the upstairs hallway spinning air through the bedrooms. But, day or night, it was hot. You would sweat in your sleep, if you could sleep at all, and wake stuck to the sheets.

I knew I should not have joined my twin friends, Connie and Joey, who at twelve were three years older than I. My mother's warnings to never play with the twins rang inside me the minute I saw them on their bikes. But when they motioned me to join them, having nothing better to do, I waited until the cars cleared on Peoria Road, then pedaled lickety-spilt to meet them.

Linda's mother, Catherine, 1949

Once inside Iocca's corner market, we headed to the donut section. Joey started cussing four-letter words. He didn't want glazed donuts; he wanted cream-filled. Connie followed by using the "s" word when she could not find raspberry-filled Bismarcks. Before long, excited by the forbidden act of swearing, I joined them, the cuss words flying out of my mouth faster than bullets.

All three of us laughed as we tried to outdo each other with bad words we had heard from the twins' parents and two older brothers. None of us paid attention to the storeowner, Mr. Iocca, wrapping meat in white butcher paper on the wooden block behind the glass refrigerated display case. I caught a glimpse of him, red-faced, shaking his head.

We settled on cream-filled chocolate bars, paid, then left the store. I saw Mr. Iocca watching us through the store window as we hopped onto our bikes. He looked upset and appeared to be talking to himself. When he turned from the store window, fading out of sight, I supposed he went to cut more meat at the back of his store. But within the hour, I would find out what he went to do.

Unknown to me, Mr. Iocca had heard from gossiping customers that the twins came from questionable family background. Both parents were known alcoholics. Their reputation as suitable guardians for their four children was negligible. Their two older sons were both current reform school residents. Neither parent seemed concerned to leave their younger children alone while they drank at the tavern up the street. Neighbors would frequently take food to the Bryan house for Connie and Joey.

One night I overheard my mom talking to Dad about the Bryans. She must not have realized I could hear her from my bedroom.

"Why, at 3:00 p.m. I couldn't believe Mrs. Bryan stumbling home so drunk!"

There was a pause, then I heard my dad's voice speak a word I didn't quite understand. He said Mom had to "*dissuade* Linda Mary from associating with the twins." My parents agreed the twins were not at fault because their parents "drank"; nevertheless, they were "inappropriate playmates."

But today, Connie, Joey, and I peddled across the street and onto the bus lane that ran the length of the fairgrounds. Racing, without holding onto our handlebars so we could eat our treats, we passed the big blue fountain inside the fairground's chain link fence. At night, multicolored lights glowed from inside this fountain, changing from yellow to red to blue to green as the water sprayed upward from a wide, shallow wading pool. When it was unbearably hot, we'd play in the fountain, squealing, splashing, and soaking ourselves under the spraying water. It felt so good to cool off before going home to bed.

We made circles and zigzags, our bikes' chrome gleaming in the sun. Sugar-buzzed we sped faster than fireflies blinking in the night and once more circled the entire bus lane. We thought moving fast would help us stay cool, until we slowed down and found ourselves drenched from the effort. I could feel my ponytail sticking to my neck while sweat slid down my back. Too hot to ride bikes, we said good-bye, then headed home in opposite directions.

I rode into our gravel driveway and onto the lawn. Jumping off my bike I sent it flying across the grass. I watched until it flipped over, wheels spinning. When the wheels began to slow, I turned toward the house, then stopped in my tracks. Mom, standing at the kitchen door, did not look happy.

Oh no, I thought, *here comes trouble!*

My heart began pounding in my throat. Fear gripped my stomach and churned my donut.

"You get in this house right now, Linda Mary," my mother ordered while holding the screen door open forcing me to step past her angry eyes.

I could feel the steaming pressure of the air rising to an oppressive level as she followed right behind me. We passed through the kitchen and into the dining room where I heard the fan whirring above the china cabinet. Grabbing my arm, Mom pulled a dining chair from the table. Jerking the chair to face the corner, she plopped me hard onto it. I winced while behind me her spitting words hissed.

"Mr. Iocca called me not ten minutes ago and told me you were swearing up a storm with the Bryan twins in his store. He said he was shocked to hear such language come from children! Now you sit there until I tell you to get up."

Mom stormed into the kitchen, banging cabinets, slamming pots and pans, muttering furiously under her breath.

It seemed I found myself sitting in the corner whenever my mother got upset because I had disobeyed, not finished my chores, or played with the twins. I could never remember my older sister, *Miss Priss,* having to endure this trial, nor did my two younger brothers seem to attract the kind of trouble I apparently had a talent for encountering.

I never meant to upset my mom. I just got caught up in what I wanted to do. Sometimes I *ignored* what she had told me, like when Connie and Joey signaled me to join them.

While my 1950s childhood was relatively carefree, my mother endured many challenges. Born two months prematurely, without hospital assistance or incubation tubes, my mom was a survivor. Like many young people during the Depression, she was determined to make her life better. Overflowing with talent, she established herself at the level of soloist in operas, operettas, and musicals while in college. An Irish Catholic and musical director at St. Aloysius Church in Springfield, she was an accomplished organist and pianist with a beautiful soprano voice. She could hit those high notes easier than I could jump off my bike at full speed. She tolerated nonsense from no one.

When I skipped piano practice, she would get upset. I knew she held expectations that I should follow in her musical footsteps. Difficult to contain my energy while sitting at the piano, I found it even harder to sing those weird arias she insisted I learn. I could barely contain my giggling when I screeched toward those high notes. She would slam her hands down on the piano, her blue eyes blazing. "Linda Mary, you are laughing on purpose!"

But I loved to sing and did so five days a week in the school choir. I had a strong voice in a brassier range than my mother's soprano talents that suited me to Broadway tunes. Tap dancing with top hat and cane, I would imitate Fred Astaire's spinning and sliding moves. Then, borrowing one of my dad's old jackets, I pinned one sleeve around my waist and held the other in my hand and did all the steps backward like Ginger Rogers did. I was in heaven. I would pedal up and down the bus lane singing Elvis tunes, watching the sunset, fantasizing about one day living in California. The Golden State, five states west from Illinois, would put me far enough away from my mother to live life on my terms.

That morning Mom had told me she wanted to rehearse in the afternoon while Dad took my two brothers to swim at the lake. My older sister, Anna Catherine, visiting relatives in Iowa, would not return until tomorrow. Standing in front of the refrigerator holding the door open to cool myself, I had said. "I want to go swim, too."

"Linda Mary, you know how easily you sunburn. You are too fair-skinned to spend the afternoon at the beach. But you can ride your bike if you promise not to stay out too long."

Mom had planned to rehearse some new musical selections. In two weeks she would perform as featured soloist at her Evening Étude ladies group. However, my episode at Iocca's had upset her plans.

A strange combination of anger at my mother and remorse for getting caught swearing overwhelmed me. Staring into the corner, my eyes moistened. The harder I bit down on my upper lip to stave off tears the more they seemed to flow. Sniveling, I stared into the white emptiness. I began to think how it might be best to run away from home and never ever return. My mother would be sorry when one day I would become famous.

My mother's insistence that I stay away from Connie and Joey would not become clear to me until I was older. Both twins would end up in the criminal courts later in life. Two bright, precocious kids, whose parents were incapable of loving them enough to establish limits or to give them guidance, would lead desperate lives.

Before long, my interests gravitated away from the twins as I engaged more in dance and the creative experience. I would come to value my mother's love and dedication to her music that inspired me to succeed in bringing my childhood dance fantasies to fruition. I would eventually teach classical ballet, modern dance, and choreography in a small California university, affirming for students the power of the arts to positively influence their lives.

During one visit to Illinois after my mom had retired at age eighty-five from over sixty years of playing masses, weddings, and funerals, I observed dust layering the grand piano. As she gestured in conversation, I noticed knobby, swollen fingers. Standing up from her chair, she wobbled unsteadily toward her kitchen or dining room. I spoke a mere decibel under yelling until sadly realizing that even with hearing aids, Mom could not hear herself sing or play the piano.

We were so alike in our temperaments, each of us finding our highest satisfaction creating beauty and joy through music and dance. We both came to believe in our own fashion that, if we were sincere in making our lives be filled with our best efforts, a hint of the sacred would always remain in our hearts.

But on that stifling summer day, as I sat facing the corner and my mother composed herself in her kitchen, our tumultuous episode began to subside.

"Linda Mary. You can get up now. Please put the chair back," she said.

As I did what she told me, I think she must have noticed my red, swollen eyes. Her expression softened. Perhaps she felt my punishment had been too severe, or so I hoped.

In a gentle but clear voice, she said to me. "Life is what you make it be, Linda Mary."

And then, my mother asked, "Would you like to come to the kitchen so together we can fix your favorite meal? You could make the hamburger patties while I cut potatoes for french fries. Cherry cobbler is in the oven. We could have everything ready by the time your father and brothers come home with the ice cream."

I looked at my mother, smiled, and together we walked into the kitchen.

SECTION TWO

Mother Loss

Introduction: *Mother Loss*

Caryn Mirriam-Goldberg

Mothers Lost and Found: The Center Ring of Who We Are

*W*hen I walked into the retirement center to facilitate an intergenerational women's writing workshop, I was astonished to find several teenagers—often labeled "the bad girls" for their propensity for drugs, drinking, sexual activity, and little tolerance for school—in the laps of women old enough to be their great-grandmothers. At that moment, I realized how much mother hunger and mother loss pervades our culture, reaching into the psyche of these girls who had lost their own mothers to bad boyfriends, bad choices, and bad circumstances. And this was also true of the elders, aching both for their lost mothers and mothering years.

During the months that followed, I witnessed acutely how distance between women and their mothers shapes every nuance of what they believe, allow themselves, and pass on to their daughters. At the same time, I saw in this workshop something that's echoed throughout the following essays: how sharing our stories can bring us wholeness, connection, and courage.

Growing up in a culture that both values and demeans mothering, we find ironic heartbreaks in most of our lives when it comes to how we claim ourselves as daughters or mothers. In the last forty years, the feminist movement has so altered what a woman can do that many of us have grown up seeking our own callings in spite of the women one generation behind us who faced severely limited choices. In the sixties, I remember playing the board game "What Shall I Be?" that listed only six careers for women: model, nurse, actress, teacher, ballet dancer, or airline hostess. Yet it was obvious that the real career choice was simply "mother." By the time I was of age, those six choices had exploded into dozens of possibilities. With such divides fueled by culture shift, the streams or rivers of enmeshment, misunderstanding, and yearning that characterize even the best mother-daughter relationships could widen into great lakes between generations. These memoirs demonstrate how such distances can be crossed or narrowed, bridged or diminished between she-who-raised-us and who we are now.

In making our way back to our mothers, we discover how much mother loss isn't just about the mother who died, but about the lives that separated us. In such reflection, we can see anew ways in which we stereotyped our own mothers and kept them at bay, often for what felt like our survival. In "Rosemary for Remembrance—Violet for Revenge," Elizabeth VanPatten tells us, "It is wise to let sleeping closets lie," a necessary step in her own evolution before she discovered the wisdom of not letting the past lie in wait for us or lie to us. Facing her demonization of her mother, she finds forgiveness for the woman her mother tried to be and greater freedom in her own life.

Understanding our mothers also means looking at the power structures of culture that often stripped our mothers from their desires. Clarice Stasz in "Edgewood" looks at how her father's decisions dampened down her mother's vitality and creativity, which she would only recover in widowhood through an eccentric life of travel. Such generational gaps, made of the black hole of self-sacrifice, also speak through Marilyn J. Curry's essay, "The Deal We Made," in which Curry finds her way to her mother through an unlikely vehicle: a television game show. Learning how to see their mothers without blame and with forgiveness, Ana Manwaring in "Not My Mother's Child" and Katrina Norfleet in "My Hero" look beyond childhood hopes and fears at how their mothers navigated a patriarchal and biased world. Such navigation skills helped both Norfleet and Manwaring achieve their own independence.

There are also the stories of losing mothers while not old enough to fly from the nest and then learning to be a woman without a guide. Deborah Jones-Norberto in "Three Mothers" illuminates the complexity and love of having three mothers: "One, chosen in grief, another lost to death, and one who created my body." Remembering the biological mother who surrendered her, the adoptive mother who died too young, and the stepmother who didn't want her, Jones-Norberto looks at the limits and limitlessness of love, and what, after the loss of all three, remains her guiding star.

Facing bittersweet and excruciating moments, Elle Tyler examines impending mother loss when her mother is given only a few weeks left to live. Tyler asks, "What was I yearning for in these last days? I know I longed for something cathartic and meaningful, something to bring us closer." In "Motherless Child," Nancy LaTurner endures a sudden loss from a great geographic distance, opening her saddened heart toward what is only reconcilable over time. Barbara Toboni in "A Moon Song" tells what it was like to be the daughter of a singer in a series of rental homes, where she grew all too well practiced at saying good-bye. Laura McHale Holland's "Little Traveler" looks into the painful loss of a mother by suicide and how to carry old pain and fresh sorrow. In all these stories of dying mothers, the authors stretch open their tattered hearts to find meaning and courage, compassion for their mothers, and passion for their own lives.

Such work of the heart often heals not only a daughter but also the generations. Tiah Marie Beautement's essay, "The Birds of Promise: A Letter to My Godmother," celebrates the transformation of a family tree cloaked with "evil intention" to a life bathed in light, in part because of the gifts of a godmother, intent on bringing a grieving child out to the wonders of the world despite her own demons.

In each essay in this section, there is the lingering song of legacy: what our mothers, grandmothers, and long generations of women left to us, and what we will do with their gifts, challenges, and stories. "Past Generations" by Nekane Polo tells the story of her mother, an idealistic young woman, and her grandmothers, unfolding legacies that speak through Polo's life today.

In each story of mother loss, we are reading the stories already written into our bodies and psyches, our pasts and futures, about what propels us into crafting, revising, and living our own life story. We carry our mothers, lost and found, in us as a tree carries its center ring at its core. Only through telling and witnessing our own and each other's stories may we find freedom from mother hunger and tenderness for mother loss and, ultimately, the love that remains.

Rosemary For Remembrance—
Violet For Revenge

Elizabeth VanPatten

*I*t is wise to let sleeping closets lie. During a rare attack of housewifery, I ignored that sensible advice and charged ahead with a clear-the-clutter campaign. In the first closet I chose for my attack, I discovered a genuine treasure lurking in the debris: the diary I kept in 1935. I settled down to read.

Who said you can't go home again? And once there my grown-up self, her own children grown and gone, was forced to confront the churlish child I was at twelve. My mother should have put me in a sack and drowned me. No jury would have convicted her. I decided to play biographer to my preteen self and expose that self-centered harpy, after correcting the atrocious spelling—my younger self frequently interrupts her scribbling to announce, "Got 100 in spelling today."

October 21, 1935
Dear Diary,

My twelfth birthday was a big fat disaster. What I wanted was a permanent. I really, really hate my dumb old straight hair. Naturally, my mother the Witch had to say that if I'd brush it 100 strokes every night it would be beautiful. She got me a stupid sensible jacket, brown, ugh, way too big so it would last longer. Got three pairs of socks to replace the ones Cubby dog chewed the toes out of. Of course, the Witch had to treat me to some of her sarcasm and say how clever it was of Cubby to know how to open my sock drawer. Stupid Neil gave me a book on spiders, which he wants to read. I hate and despise spiders. And I couldn't blow out all the candles on my cake because guess who put a candle on that wouldn't blow out. Now I won't get my wish, but since it was about Billy Wallace, I probably wouldn't get it anyway. Aunt Beth sent this diary. She is one of Daddy's sisters. I've never met her. I guess maiden ladies think girls my age still write stupid stuff in diaries. She doesn't realize I'm not a child anymore. Decided I would write in it just so I wouldn't have to tell a lie when I write to thank her. Actually, it's kind of fun, sort of.

Elizabeth with her mother and brother, 1932

I just had a brilliant idea! I'll start my diary by telling the story of how my mother, brother, and I happen to be here in California and not in Alaska anymore.

I was born in Alaska, which makes me a Sourdough and not a Chechakho like the rest of my family. They were born somewhere else, even my stupid brother. For some reason, when I was six years old my mother left Daddy in Alaska and brought Neil and me to live in California. I remember the trip down the Inside Passage in a huge boat that took us to San Francisco. The Witch's sister, Aunt Helen, and her husband met us with their car. They took us to live at their house in Modesto, a couple of hours east of San Francisco. I had never been in a car before because there were board streets and no cars in Alaska. Riding in that Model A Ford was fun, but not as much fun as the speedboat I was used to.

We lived with Aunt Helen until the Witch finally found a house for us. It was okay, but I had to share a bedroom with stupid Neil, ugh.

Anyway, I'm glad we came to California six years ago because now that I'm twelve and in the eighth grade, I'll get to go to junior high school next year, where Billy Wallace is. I just know I'm going to have a lot of good stuff to tell my diary!

July 10, 1936

I'm cried out—my face is so blotchy I look like a boiled pig. The Witch says we are moving to some stupid town called Yuba City, about a zillion miles north of here—well four hours, anyway—where she got a better job. If Billy Wallace saw me now he'd probably throw up, not that he knows I'm alive. I'm not going to get to go to junior high school and I've been waiting practically my whole life to go, especially now that Billy Wallace is there. I was planning to maybe bump into him in the hall and he'd say, "Oh, sorry, did I hurt you? Would you like some gum?" and he'd offer me a stick of Juicy Fruit. I know that's his favorite because I picked up a wrapper he dropped last year (I have it in my treasure box) when he was still here at grade school.

July 12, 1936

I'm still crying. How can I leave all my friends, Janie, Eloise, Margot, Patty, and go off to live in some country town full of hicks and hickettes, no junior high school and no Billy Wallace? I think I'm going to kill myself. If only I didn't have trouble swallowing pills; I'm afraid of heights, the sight of blood makes me woozy, and the smell of gas is just disgusting. But that's okay because I'm going to die of a broken heart, or maybe tuberculosis. One of Daddy's sisters died of that. I didn't ever meet any of his family, and now he doesn't live with us anymore and I'm left with the Witch and stupid Neil. I don't think the Witch was ever a girl who wanted to go to junior high school so much she would just about die if she couldn't.

July 15, 1936

Still crying. This whole moving mess wouldn't have happened if only we had stayed in Alaska and not left Daddy. Actually, my mother wasn't a witch until we left Alaska.

A month or so after we moved to California I was coming back from my new friend Janie's, and there was Daddy sitting on a dining room chair on the sidewalk in front of the house. I was so happy to see him, but he looked awfully mad and didn't pay any attention to me. I turned around and went back to Janie's. Nobody ever told me anything about why he was there and I didn't ask. I do think probably someone got in trouble for taking a dining room chair outside. I got scolded just for taking the cushions off the living room couch to make a little house for my dolls. If stupid Neil did that—not that he would ever touch my dolls, and he better not—nobody would say anything to him. It's not fair! I can just hear the Witch saying, as she always does, "Fair is the first syllable of fairy tale."

July 20, 1936

All I want to do is stay in bed and write in my diary. That's the only thing that helps. I keep thinking about the last time I saw Daddy, when we were still at Aunt Helen's house. I wish I had told him I was glad to see him. Maybe he wouldn't have been so mad. Maybe he would have stayed here and everything would be all right again. The Witch wouldn't have to work so she wouldn't be tired all the time and she would be nicer. Well, I'm really tired now and I need to sleep. The Witch is still at work. She said I should start dinner—peel the potatoes and pick some chard from the backyard. Maybe my heart will break while I'm asleep and I won't have to peel the stupid potatoes. I despise chard.

August 2, 1936

The Witch got a letter saying Daddy is dead. He came down with measles, which turned into pneumonia and he died. Before he died, though, he sent a package that had a big turtle and a horned toad in it, so we knew he was somewhere by a desert. There was a book of poems with my name on it and his handwriting in the margins by poems he liked, saying I will understand them some day and I will love them.

September 15, 1936

We have moved and I hate it! I hate it! I hate it! I just bit my arithmetic book but it didn't help. This is an ugly town full of boring people and only one dinky little movie theater and no junior high school. The teachers at my new school are okay. I've never had men teachers before and I like my teacher, Mr. Onstott. He has curly blond hair and a dimple. I think he hates this place, too, because I've seen him standing at the window and he looks sad.

The girl who sits in front of me is Violet and I think she's an Okie. She has frizzy hair and her neck is dirty, also her feet. She doesn't wear any socks, just sandals, and her dress—I think she has only one—the Witch wouldn't even use for a dust rag. She is always quiet, even at recess and nobody talks to her. Maybe she has a dog that eats all her socks, not just the toes the way Cubby does. Every time I think of that day, before we moved, when the teacher told us to take off our shoes for a foot inspection, I still blush. There I was in my chewed-up socks. I wish I'd died right then and gotten it over with.

September 20, 1936

The Witch informed me that she met a lady who has a daughter my age and she said Harriet, her stupid daughter, would be getting in touch with me. I didn't say anything because I am not talking at home, not that the Witch takes any notice. That's all I need, some moron being nice because her mother told her to. Yuck and double yuck. I will definitely ignore her.

November 10, 1936

Things are not getting any better. Mr. Onstott scolded me for not paying attention. I was thinking about how to get revenge on the Witch, so of course I wasn't paying attention to boring arithmetic. Mr. Onstott has a big old bald spot and his dimple is really more of a wrinkle. Every book I've ever read says when the bad guy hurts the good guy, it's time for revenge. I would like to hurt the Witch the way she hurt me. What I need is an idea of what to do to punish her. In the meantime, I'm going to cut into that cake she told us not to because she's taking it to some gruesome meeting. It will make her mad, but she won't say anything because she's trying to be nice as pie. I think she feels bad about my not having junior high school to look forward to—if witches can feel bad, which I doubt. They say revenge is sweet, but first you have to think up a way to get it. Revenge, that is. It's not fair, and I know what the Witch would say about that.

November 15, 1936

I've got it! I know how I'm going to get my revenge on the Witch! She's always going on about the "right" people, and every time we mention someone new, she wants to know what their father does, where they live. I think it's really dumb. Anyway, I know for sure she wouldn't like Violet, so I'm going to make her my new best friend! I talked to her at recess and she is awfully shy, but she has pretty eyes and her smile would be pretty, too, if she didn't have teeth that look like they need a lot of work. She is from Oklahoma and her family lives in their car. They all work in whatever crops are being picked. I'm going to ask her to Thanksgiving dinner! Aunt Helen, Uncle Dode, and my two cousins are going to drive up here to this stupid town. I like Aunt Helen, but she is just as bad as the Witch when it comes to the "right" people. It makes me feel better just thinking about seeing the Witch's face when she sees Violet.

November 26, 1936

Thanksgiving dinner was a big success, although I think I won't have to eat for a month. I was surprised at how nice Mother was to Violet. She talked to her a lot and smiled at her and said nice things about her hair. I did catch the cousins giggling when they saw the price tag dangling from the back of Violet's dress. I didn't know Woolworth's even sold dresses. I gave the cousins my best bad look. I thought Violet looked really pretty. She didn't say much, which is just as well because she does have an Okie drawl. I hope she had a good time. Violet is sweet when you get to know her. I'm feeling bad that I used her to get revenge. I think I'm beginning to understand Mother better. In fact, I'm not going to call her the Witch anymore in my diary. She has had too many bad things happen and I definitely haven't been any help.

December 15, 1936

Harriet invited me to a Christmas party at her home. I don't know what I'll wear because I don't have a party dress. I begged and begged Mother to buy me one and she said "We'll see," which isn't "No" so I'll keep working on her.

Harriet took me to see a play that was put on at her church and it was lots of fun. I'm going to join her Bible study group. I can hardly wait for next summer because Harriet's family has a swimming pool. She said it's out by the cherry orchard and we can swim and eat all the cherries we want. I wonder if Harriet's mother thinks I'm one of the "right" people?

Violet said today she wouldn't be coming to school anymore because her Daddy said they have to move on and find work. She said she would try to send me a postcard from Los Angeles. I will miss her.

The memories rekindled by reading these sometimes grubby, tear-stained pages are forcing me to take another look at my mother. I wonder, as I finish clearing out the forgotten closet, if I had been placed in her position, would I have been able to be an all-loving, patient *Little Women* kind of mother? Looking back on my own comfortable life as full-time mother, with excellent support from my husband, was I the wise, kind, and perfect mother that I expected my mother to be? She seems to have been singled out to carry a heavy load, but she refused to let it crush her, in spite of a hateful daughter. Belatedly, I forgive her, as well as her daughter, who enjoys a new level of understanding.

No Tears

Elle Tyler

*W*hen the doctor told my mother that she had two to three weeks to live, it took my breath away and my eyes immediately filled up with tears. After the doctor left the room to gather the latest test results, I turned to my mother. She looked up at me, and with her old familiar voice of a drill sergeant, barked, "No tears!" Even in the face of her ultimate departure, I was not allowed to cry.

I had never seen my mother cry. She had been through multiple surgeries in her life: a hysterectomy, gallbladder removal, hernia and parathyroid operations, and, ultimately, a double mastectomy. She had nursed my father through a life-threatening heart attack and my brother through infectious hepatitis, all while trying to help me to deal with the loss of my unborn child. She had never cried; never shed a tear. Never wallowed in fear or dread or negativity. At least, I never saw any display of emotion. Was the 5:00 p.m. scotch an attempt to cover, conceal, or protect her heart? She would say, "No, it was social," that she liked the taste, never that it might have dulled the pain or taken the edge off the fear. She was a survivor . . . always bigger than life.

But now, here she sat in a wheelchair. It was 2005 and we were in the best hospital in New York City. They offered an experimental drug treatment: forty volunteers so far, pages of devastating side effects but a chance for remission, to live for a little longer—a day, a month, a year—it was anybody's guess. There were no guarantees. She took the gamble. Without missing a beat, she signed on, and I wheeled her up to her room where she put on the hospital gown and settled in for eight weeks of chemotherapy. The medical procedures were endless: tests to examine her lungs, colon, blood, urine, heart, kidneys, liver, and bladder. Specialists were called in to interpret her blurry vision, scratchy throat, and mouth full of sores. Day after day, an array of doctors, nurses, physical therapists, volunteers, and teams of specialists surrounded her and tried to put the pieces of her medical puzzle together.

I would sit in a chair by her side watching her sleep. Observing her breath, always labored, I scanned her fragile body, full of bruises and sores.

Elle and her mother, circa 1995

My mother had lived a suburban lifestyle with country club values. Appearance was important to her. She had been a full-figured woman who exuded an elegant style. She made weekly trips to the beauty parlor to keep her strawberry blonde hairdo perfectly in place. Although she was not a classic beauty, she did everything she could to enhance her appearance. She had a deep and powerful voice that projected authority and leadership. Many of her friends looked up to and depended on her. But now she was no longer "commander in chief." She was so tiny lying in that bed.

What was I yearning for in these last days? I know I longed for something cathartic and meaningful, something to bring us closer. In between her naps we would reminisce, and sometimes in the silence I would watch her eyes appear to glaze over. At those moments I waited, anticipating something profound or nostalgic . . . a memory or a question. I would reach for her hand and sit patiently until the words formulated in her mind. And then she would look into my eyes, and with complete focus and concentration she would ask me, "What happened to your highlights?" or "When did you get a stomach?" or some other external observation. It never failed to surprise me that she could be in such a weakened state and still notice and comment on a physical imperfection.

When I was a child, my mother had always picked out my wardrobe and encouraged me to straighten my naturally curly hair. We had many arguments concerning my appearance. My mother was a product of the affluent community she lived in, surrounded by ladies who lunched and played golf, while nannies cared for their children. They also contributed to charities and created beautiful homes for their families. They projected sophistication and success.

But I was an artist, and eventually I found a different style. Being an artist gave me permission to transcend the rigid glossy boundaries of the suburbs in search of what was authentic to me. So, at these moments with my mother, I had to laugh. I couldn't be defensive anymore. I had to accept that the level of our communication might never be what I had longed for. But, day after day, I came in hoping to transcend our limitations.

I often wondered what my life would have been like if my mother had truly understood me. What if she could have valued my innate sensitivity and guided me to channel it in creative ways? What if she could have realized my childhood outbursts were more a cry to be understood than an attempt to be defiant? She always called me "Sarah Bernhardt," but not in a complimentary way. If she had only known that my intense emotions were not a curse but my greatest gift. I needed a mother who would let me cry and even cry with me, a mother who would honor, respect, and appreciate me.

There were moments when I got a glimpse of what that felt like. Before being hospitalized, she had allowed me to direct her into my world of holistic healing. When I was twenty-seven, I was stricken with rheumatoid arthritis. My mother connected me to the top specialist in the field, but the very kind and prestigious doctor was only able to offer me a prescription for fifteen aspirin a day. He calmly stated that I had a "degenerative and progressive" disease that could only get worse. That was a defining moment in my life. I became a vegetarian and with meditation, fasting, and herbs within the year I had healed myself. Sadly, my greatest triumph alienated me even further from my mother. We no longer ate the same foods or lived the same lifestyle.

However, toward the end of her life, when all else appeared to fail, she opened up to my world. Without words, her actions validated my belief system. She accompanied me to my Chinese doctor, who prescribed special herbs to bolster her immune system. She then came to meet a cancer specialist who prescribed countless supplements along with a meditation tape with instructions on visualization. She did it all. She followed my lead. I would like to believe these treatments gave her the extra time that she had. I will never know, but during those times I felt validated. Sometimes I reflected on how far we had come in our acceptance and appreciation of each other. It may have happened late in our relationship, but that was better than not at all.

My days with my mother in the hospital started to blend into each other. The corridors leading to her room were all too familiar. I felt the energy drain from my body as I made my way down the long, dark hallway, anticipating what I would see when I opened the door. Would she be sitting up, alert and eager for my visit, or lying down attached to the oxygen mask and IV tubes? My heartbeat always quickened as I entered the room. I thought, yes, it's a new day and my mother is alive . . . her will to live still stronger than any stray leukemia cells trying to ambush her body.

I suspected she made the choice to live because she was not ready to leave my father. They both knew it was not supposed to end this way. Quite frankly, I think she felt he would be lost without her. My father had reinvented himself three times during their marriage: from a college professor to a wholesale liquor distributor and now, at eighty-seven, completing forty-one years as an investment counselor at Smith Barney.

He loved to work. And she loved taking care of him, all the little details, from having food on the table to making his doctor's appointments and filling his prescriptions. She had total control over their social calendar and packed his bag when they traveled. My father had never toasted a bagel or scrambled an egg. How could he survive without her? He was always her first priority. And she was his.

When she was hospitalized, Dad showed up every day and sat by her bedside. He was a quiet man with a sharp wit and loving sense of humor. They had always stuck together, like an impenetrable fortress. When I had arguments with my mother, my father wouldn't speak to me until I apologized to her, even when it wasn't my fault. They lived for each other. And so she decided to endure anything and everything that the doctors prescribed. She never questioned, and completely trusted their judgment.

Because of the uncertainty of her condition, my brothers flew in every few months. We would sit around her bed and she would delegate. She didn't want the top of the line when we bought the casket . . . but still something special. My brother said, "You mean you don't want the Mercedes, you want the Lexus?" She said, "Exactly." We talked about her obituary and funeral service and precious belongings that she wanted us to share. Even in what appeared to be her last days, my mother was completely lucid and in total control. When she finished talking, she asked us to go down the street and buy her a chocolate milkshake. She needed to close her eyes and rest. We never spoke of those arrangements again.

The days and weeks passed slowly. The diagnosis and treatment were constantly changing, optimism and hope turning to fear and sadness. Days filled with the unknown, no answers, just an endless array of questions. Then my mother made the decision to go home.

Like my mother, I too had made a choice, to be there with her. It was easy to put a halt on other activities. This was my priority. I was going on this journey with her. She was going to have me by her side, day and night, giving her my warmth, understanding, and love. She would have, at her death, what I couldn't claim at my birth. As I rubbed my mother's parched and calloused feet, the intimacy of touch seemed strangely unfamiliar. Had she ever wrapped her arms around me or cradled me close to her heart? It didn't matter now. I knew my mother loved me and had done her best. At that moment, all our misunderstandings were forgiven. I was able to see my mother as separate from myself, and all my longing to be understood and validated dissipated. My mother was going to die without ever questioning her life. She would pass knowing she had done her best, and I would know that, too.

The day my mother died, she called me early in the morning. Her voice was weak but steady as she told me that she loved me. "Please don't mourn me," she said. "You must celebrate my life." I hung up the phone and rushed to her apartment, wanting a chance to see her one last time. I hoped that she would tell me again that she loved me, or maybe elaborate on all the things that were special about me. When I arrived, the hospice nurse opened the door and told me my mother was still alive. I quickly composed myself, losing any trace of sadness. "Hi, Mom," I said, with a big smile as I entered her room.

"Here comes the actress," she said. Her breathing was labored, but she could still make a joke. She knew I was acting.

She would have it her way. There would be No Tears.

We gathered around her bed. She asked my father to take out her jewelry. She went through each piece and designated who would receive it. She then had my brother take out a few of her sweat suits, and she picked the one she wanted to be buried in. My mother, who had always dressed elegantly, chose to be buried in a casual jogging suit. She preferred the casket to be closed. Social status and image no longer mattered.

My back hurt that day and I crawled onto her bed, complaining like a little child. I just wanted to be close to her. With all the strength she could muster, she took a moment to rub my back. That tender gesture was the acceptance I had always needed from her. There were no more words, confessions, or shared memories. My mother's spirit was waning. She took off her wedding ring and gave it to me. Our hands were clasped together as she took her last breath.

They say we choose our parents: that we each fulfill some karmic lesson. I realize now that my mother wanted more than anything else for me to exhibit strength and independence. She tried to teach me in the best way she knew how. We were made from different cloth, but we went through this life together. I suppose we both taught each other important lessons, but my mother never articulated that she learned anything from me. Somehow, in my heart, I hope she did.

Looking back on my mother's life, I realize there were many qualities I did appreciate about her. She was strong and loyal to her family and friends. She was controlling, but she always came through in a crisis. She had always been generous with me in a material way. Nothing made her happier than taking me shopping or lending me her best silver if I was having a party. Her values were ensconced in the material world and because of her generosity I was able to pursue my dreams in acting and drama therapy. Living through my mother's illness and death, I experienced her strength and resilience. She never complained. She went through every procedure and all the setbacks like a warrior. And when she made her final decision to stop the experimental treatments, she did so with dignity and not a trace of fear. Strength, Generosity, Loyalty, and Love: I know these parts of her live on in me . . . and always will.

The Deal We Made

Marilyn J. Curry

One of the last television shows my mother fell for was *Deal or No Deal*, a game show hosted by Howie Mandel, where the contestants pick one unopened briefcase that they believe has their million dollars. There are no questions to the game, no competition, just the fascination of watching people who seemingly don't have much money pass up six-digit amounts in the belief they have picked the million. The show was a hit, and my mother, who always knew the show business back stories, got a kick out of Howie having a comeback. Apparently he needed it.

My mother was always an in-the-know kind of a person when it came to movie and television personalities, but in the last phase of her illness, virtually housebound, she had limited options. When my brother and I saw her watching reruns of *Dr. Quinn, Medicine Woman*, we tried to talk her into cable, of course offering to pay. She insisted that the broadcast networks were enough. I had never been a television person, but I crossed over. At first it was a way to visit with my mother, then it was something to talk about when we were apart, and now there really is no excuse.

I can be entertained by shows that I'd never dreamed of watching, like *Dancing with the Stars*. (My mother loved Cheryl Burke.) When I sit in front of the television in my home in San Francisco, content in a way that I don't recognize, I ask my husband if he finds it odd that I am so drawn to the tube. He says he thinks it is a way of being close to my mother.

My mother was diagnosed with multiple myeloma, an incurable cancer, in 2002, and I began a series of visits to Queens, New York, as if it were a trip around the corner. While in her home, when I wasn't doing the chores that she always saved for me—

washing the chandelier globes, dusting the blades of the ceiling fan, getting a repairman to fix the back door that only locked with a hook—I took my place in a Queen Anne chair in the dining room next to my mother, who sat in her recliner and watched television.

It was a cozy room with lace curtains and tablecloth, a mahogany china cabinet and bureau, and a television set that still had an antenna. I was never comfortable sitting in my chair for very long; it gave me back pain. But my mother, who suf-

Eleanor and Marilyn, 1988

fered from a lot of pain, found comfort in sitting. I preferred lying on the living room floor, engaged in yoga stretches. From the floor I could still see my mother and hear her television, while watching a smaller set with the sound off.

We did all right until the commercials came on. Then she would turn to talk to me, and I couldn't concentrate on what she was saying because the escalated volume of the Swiffer commercials went right through me. The first few days of my visits I didn't ask her to mute the commercials; I toughed it out. I was trying not to be "sensitive," which was, according to her, the main reason for our long history of not "getting along." By the middle of the visit, when I was more worn down, I asked her to mute the sound, and she said, "You're a pain in the ass." By the end, when I saw my mother pick up the remote and press the mute button before she talked to me, my heart tugged because I knew she wanted to get it right, we both did, before it was time for me to leave again.

On one visit my mother had just been released from the hospital after a bout of pneumonia and could not walk from her recliner in the dining room to the kitchen without holding on with both hands to the surrounding furniture. She still refused hired help.

"I'm fine," she said. "I don't want strangers sitting around in this house."

Near the end of the visit, I said to my brother on the phone, "It is so hard for me to leave her. I have to believe she can make it by herself."

"Well, the truth is she can't. But, even if you lived here in New York, you wouldn't be living with her unless there was something wrong with you." We both laughed.

My brother's joke about women who never left their mothers being odd or impaired was from our childhood. I remember visiting one of my grandmother's old friends in the Bushwick section of Brooklyn when I was a child. The rooms were dark with old smells of cooked cabbage and stale birdseed for the blue parakeet. Other than the candy dishes I was afraid to touch, there was Mrs. Shulbach, with her wire-rimmed glasses and gray bun, and her daughter Rose. There were no husbands, no children—just two grown women living together. Rose spoke in a kind, childlike voice to me, and I could see the hair on her legs and the white socks, and I wanted to hide. Later, coming home on the bus, my grandmother referred to Rose as a "blessing" to her mother.

> It is 1976—I am sitting at the gray Formica table in my grandmother's kitchen and my mother is complaining about her mother. My mother has moved back in with her mother and has been living with her for a year. I am twenty-six and my mother is fifty-two.
>
> "She drives me crazy," my mother erupts, "I can't take the guilt tripping." This is the first time I hear that phrase coming from her.
>
> It is spring and I have cajoled my mother into opening the windows to counteract the rumblings of the old refrigerator and the ticking of the electric clock, while I record her voice for a film. The film is about the messages my mother and grandmother gave me about men and marriage. I live in

San Francisco with my women friends and I have been studying in the film department at the university with the ambition
of changing the image of women in the media. In truth, I am
more involved with changing myself.

She looks at me intensely. "Don't do this, girl; stay in
California. I have no freedom. Your life is never your own
once you take care of a parent."

She takes out the butter for the bread. "I don't have any
of those soy spreads." She is referring to my eating habits. "I
have to give Grandma her perm today."

Later I film my mother as she holds a pink plastic curler in
her mouth as my grandmother hands her the tissue paper to
fold over her hair.

My mother, an only child, gave up the apartment she loved
and moved back with her mother after her father died, because
she couldn't let her live alone. My grandmother was able-bodied
and my mother lived only a block away. The move back into her
mother's home resulted in a complete loss of privacy. My mother,
who was widowed at thirty-two, had started dating in her forties.
For nine years before moving back in with her mother, she had
a steady boyfriend whom she accompanied on vacations. After
the move, when the vacations continued, my grandmother complained about being left alone. The guilt infuriated my mother.

When my mother moved in with my grandmother, I didn't ask
why. In my twenties, it wasn't a question fully formed in my mind.
But after she died I talked to her close friend Pat, who lived across
the street and worked with my mother in the dentist office for thirty
years. Pat was a just a few years older than me and lived around the
corner from her mother. The only response Pat could offer when
I asked how my mother felt about moving in was a phrase that I
heard often in my neighborhood, "You do what you have to do."

One evening after dinner during one of my visits I carried a
tub of hot water to my mother to soak her feet, and she reflected,
"I used to soak Grandma's feet on Friday nights, after a dinner
of fish sticks, her favorite." I could hear in my mother's voice a

peacefulness that I rarely heard when she talked about the years of living with her own mother. I was happy for her; she could see herself as a good daughter. My mother never enjoyed enough of a life without resentment and, at the same time, she felt she had not done enough for her mother. And my grandmother never understood the sacrifice my mother made, the loss of privacy. To her, the move into her house represented a gift to her daughter. In a letter my grandmother sent me, she wrote, "Your mother will never have to move again. She will have her own place."

In 2006, after a visit with my mother, I came home to San Francisco and went by myself to the historic Castro Theatre to see the re-released documentary film, *Grey Gardens*. In the 1970s when I first saw the film, I was embarking on a career as a documentary filmmaker in San Francisco. I thought of my own mother and grandmother back in the same house again. My mother was stronger than Little Edie, but there were similarities: two adult women living under the same roof; a mother and daughter bickering constantly, but bound by the strongest relationship they would ever know.

Sitting in the Castro Theatre thirty years later, I was surprised how close I felt to Little Edie when she said, "I had to come home. I had to take care of my mother." Even if she was eccentric, possibly mentally ill, with a sweater wrapped around her head as a fashionable turban, I could see her as a daughter like myself compelled by the need to take care of her mother.

After that day at the Castro, there was one more year of visits. Some of them were harrowing, filled with urgent medical needs, complications from chemo, terrifying congestive heart failure emergencies when my mother almost died in front of me. But when my mother was stable, she and I had the leisurely pleasure of a lunch at London Lennie's, with crunchy cole slaw and good bread, or a trip to the hairdresser, where my mother's spirits were lifted by a new perm. We hung wash, sorted mail, paid bills, and ate meals together. At times tempers flared, old battles emerged as if I were a teenager again, but we didn't dig in, we let it go. Each night before I went upstairs to bed I would kiss my mother on the cheek; half the time she would be asleep with the television roaring and I would check to see if she was still breathing.

In between visits I went back home to my husband and my job. When I was in my own light-filled San Francisco house, sometimes it took me days to feel at home, to recognize my life with my husband as my own. The visits with my mother in the house where she grew up, on the block where I grew up, in the small residential neighborhood in Queens, became the life that felt the most real. The lure of Manhattan, the "city" as people in Queens referred to it, the place that held my first memories of sophistication, anonymity, culture, and escape faded away.

With each visit my mother grew frailer, but held on to her independence, only letting me hire part-time help in the last six months. She and I, who had lived 3,000 miles apart for so long, now took such pleasure in each other's company. "Don't do what I did," she had said. I hadn't. I left to make a life of my own. But at the end I had the immense, poignant comfort of being back home with my mother and she had her daughter.

My mother spent the last five days of her life in a hospice in the Bronx. It was the end of January, a gray, cold time. The night before she died I came home from visiting her. She had been put on morphine and lost consciousness that afternoon. I was alone in her house, cold. I wrapped myself in her black car coat and sat in her recliner and turned on the television. It was *Deal or No Deal*. I called the front desk to check on her. The helpful woman said, "She is resting comfortably."

"I had her favorite show on and I had to call."

"It's on in her room, too."

A year later I sold my mother's house. I had gone back three more times to carefully sort through all of her possessions. Some of the furniture was left in the house for the new owner, including my mother's recliner. Before I closed the door for the last time, I stood in front of my mother's chair and said out loud, "If I could do it all over again, I would never leave you." In that moment, it felt true.

Past Generations

Nekane Polo

My mother was only fourteen and full of hopes and dreams when she entered the boarding school in Zaragoza, Spain, where she hoped to graduate and then become a nun. Since childhood that was all she had wanted to do. Later, she claimed that her time there was the happiest of her life. She had fond memories of her school days, and she often told us children about them. She recalled how cold it was, and how hard she worked, but also she told us about the fun and laughter that she shared with her friends. She was proud of the high standard of education she achieved there, which included piano and etiquette lessons as well as her academic subjects. As we grew older, she would teach us about setting a table properly, making polite conversation, and walking on high heels. But after four years at school, she was told that due to her poor health, she would not be eligible to become a nun.

Heartbroken and not knowing what to do next, Mum returned home where, taking her mother's advice, she completed a secretarial course, leading to a job in the city of Bilbao. This was an opportunity for Mother to embrace life and do the exciting things that young women did in those days, like going to dances or the cinema, and even sharing the same train with friends on their way to work.

Her capabilities soon gained her a personal assistant position. It was through work that she met a friend of her boss whom she married a few months later. She accepted that this is what God had planned for her and devoted herself to her husband and children. She confined herself to her home and, being a shy, quiet young woman, it took several years for her to even meet the neighbors in the block of apartments where she lived in Bilbao.

Children go about their business not knowing what's going on around them; for me and my three brothers, it was normal to see our mum at home every day. We never questioned why she didn't go out more often. Sometimes I remember we even got angry when she took afternoon tea next door and was five minutes late coming back. To us it was normal to see our granny bring the groceries every day—and this was done partially because my mum preferred it that way, but also because when she went out, my dad wanted to know where she had been and with whom.

Nekane (right) and her mum in London, 1987

Every day my mum would do her housework in the morning; in the afternoon she would sit and embroider and listen to all our tales about school, friends, and so on. I remember how excited we used to get when it was baking day and we would all help to make cookies. On our birthdays she would bake us a cake and put on a wonderful spread of afternoon tea for us to share with our friends.

Despite my father having his own business and our family being quite well off, my mother had a very modest budget for the housekeeping because my father thought that running a home with four children only involved buying food. My brothers and I would often watch my mother and grandmother undertake several industrious tasks, like making a new cover for the sofa, wallpapering the living room, or making clothes for us. Of course, we thought that they just liked doing these things, when in reality my grandmother was helping my mother to run a more cost efficient home.

When I think about it, I realize that these women belonged to a generation when women did all the work without complaining. In contrast, my younger generation just went to school and sat in front of the television for the rest of the day, only clearing up the table under heavy protest. My grandmother, who was a seamstress, didn't know about "me time," and she was always on my case about doing something productive while I watched television. Couldn't I at least sew at the same time? Of course not! I belonged to a different generation, the television one. We were incapable of doing two things at the same time. Having said that, she did love playing cards, and when there was nothing else to do, meaning no more work and usually late at night, she would urge my mum to sit down and play. If Mum said that she had washing to do, my grandmother would reply, "What washing? The washing machine does that!" She'd always win the argument.

When I was seven, my father decided to move my family to Madrid to start a new business, but it didn't work and we had to return home. He did the same thing when I was nineteen, but this time he sold our home and, when the business didn't work, we had to move into his mother's house. He then moved my grandmother and her sister-in-law, with whom she lived, into a small apartment in Bilbao.

In fairness to Dad, he was trying to build a future for us with a business that we could take over when we were ready—which my brothers did later on. But in the meantime, my mother always supported my father against her better judgment; all the money that the business made was always put back into it, leaving my mother with less and less money. She started to do her own hair and stopped going out for coffee, which she had only done once a week with her two neighbors, relegating this only to special occasions.

But none of this we noticed as children, because our father was very generous with us and financially supported us until we got married. He used to close his business for the whole month of July every year to take us to the south of Spain where we rented and apartment with a swimming pool. My mother taught us how to rinse our swimming suits to take the salt and chlorine out of them and, always knowing what we had covered in school, she took every opportunity to incorporate some lessons into our sightseeing. Beach in the mornings, lunch in restaurants, swimming pool in the afternoons—our memories of these holidays are fantastic.

My mother's health was never great. She had several operations, but this is another thing that we never noticed as children because she kept going and, with the help of both my grandmothers, our daily routine never changed.

When I was eleven, my father's brother came to live with us. He had cirrhosis and the doctors had sent him home, saying that there was nothing else they could do for him. He had immigrated to America some years before, but had nobody to look after him there. My father decided to bring him to our house where Dad hoped his brother would get better. Indeed, thanks to my mother who nursed him day and night, he lived another thirty years.

Our home was a three-bedroom apartment and it was already overcrowded with six of us, so I had to give up my bedroom for my uncle and went to sleep in a sofa bed in the living room for the next nine years. I don't remember this being a traumatic experience because my mother was very good at defusing awkward situations and always making us feel loved.

Ours was a busy household, with seven of us living together and with both grannies, our granddad, and my great-aunt popping in and out on a daily basis. Often they stayed with us on the weekends. Understandably, Mum was very busy and always tried to please everyone, but she always seemed to have time for us, keeping in tune with everything we were doing and providing advice and support. She made time for her husband, of course, talked to the grannies, and kept in touch with the neighbors.

Even with all the family members needing her attention, Mum cared for her neighbors as well. Her neighbor and best friend had her fifth child when she was forty-eight years old, and this came as a great shock to her, leading to postnatal depression. My mother used to go down to her to get her out of bed by pretending that it was her turn to provide the afternoon tea that day, and most of the time was successful.

Here is another thing that I don't understand about my generation: despite having all the modern conveniences, we don't seem to have time to spend with our children, let alone visit friends and family. We run around like headless chickens and we are all stressed out. Stress is another of those words that my mother and grandmother did not have in their vocabulary, like the "me time" word.

I remember one summer when my children were young. I went to spend a couple of weeks with my parents. By then I had moved to England and only saw them once a year. Being a mother did not come naturally to me and when I mentioned that I didn't seem to have any time for myself, my mother laughed and said, "What did you expect with three young children to take care of?"

I envy women of those generations who got married and were happy to stay at home and look after their families. It seems to me that nowadays we are never happy. If we are at home, we want to be out working, and if we work outside the home, we feel guilty and want to stay at home. Why is it that we can't achieve the contentment and happiness that they used to have?

My grandmother, like everyone in those days, used to say that your health is your wealth: If you have that, a roof over your head, a good husband, and children, what more do you want? I don't know what we want, but some of us haven't found it yet. I think we should reflect more on the wisdom of women from past generations and learn from them.

I left home when I was twenty years old, leaving my mother at home with five men. And as the years went on, instead of her workload getting lighter, it got heavier. My grannies got older and Mum had to look after them. She used to go to my granny's house and do her hair, nails, and so on, so even if Granny didn't go anywhere she would still be presentable. Mum lived nearby so she could pop in a few times a week and make sure that Granny and her sister-in-law had everything they needed. But when it was her parents' turn, Mum had to take two busses. She didn't drive and this was a bit more difficult since she had to make sure she was home when the men came back for their lunch, as is customary in Spain.

My father went around to see his mother on a regular basis, but as her health deteriorated he went less often until he stopped going altogether. It was left to my mother to look after her and my great-aunt when they got sick. My mum and her sister-in-law took turns to nurse them both in their final days. They died within a month of each other and my mum's conscience was clear, as she was there when they passed away.

I was married and already had my first daughter when it was time for my father to retire. Despite my brothers being involved in the business, Dad was used to being in control of everything; the idea of losing that control is what I think led to him have a nervous breakdown. Once again, it was thanks to my mum, who had managed to save five thousand pounds, that my dad was able to spend a couple of weeks in a private hospital. This helped a bit, but when he came back there were days when he didn't take his medication and he was very difficult to live with. Mum endured this nightmare for another ten years before, against all her beliefs, she finally divorced Dad.

For a woman who had never lived on her own before, this was incredibly difficult, and it took her some years to get used to it. In the meantime, her father, who had always been her world, died of a heart attack, leaving Mum devastated. Eventually, she made some friends and met the man with whom she would share the rest of her life. At last, she had some freedom and happiness, but her freedom was not long-lived. Her ninety-year old mother was too fragile to continue living on her own, so Mum brought her to live with them.

My grandmother was an incredibly strong woman, whose mind was still sharp at that age. Given her love of playing cards, she could still keep count of everything on the table and won most of the time. Always proud of her appearance, she would color-coordinate her clothes and shoes to match her outfit, as well as putting on a bit of lipstick even if she was just going out for a walk around the neighborhood. She would often tell me about how she used to dye her shoes and handbag to match the outfit that she had made herself when she was young. She said everybody thought that she had money because she was so well turned out. I loved to sit with her and listen to how different her life had been in comparison to mine. With no water in the house, wooden floors to sand down, five children to look after, and working from home as a seamstress, she definitely had no "me time." My mother looked after my grandmother for another eight years until she peacefully passed away in her arms.

It's true what they say, that they don't make women like they used to. There is something comforting in learning about the lives of our mothers and grandmothers, and I have nothing but respect for women of past generations. One of the things that I admire most from my past generations of women is their perseverance. And when modern life is stressing me out, I keep going and remember that there is "no such thing as I can't, but I can and I will."

My Hero

Katrina Norfleet

The summer of 1980 my mother and I headed north on Interstate 95, traveling back home to New York from my college orientation in Washington, D.C. Until that day in the cramped confines of a two-door Ford sedan, my mother had never shared her opinion with me about anything close to an intimate relationship.

We had exited the dimly lit Baltimore Harbor tunnel, readying for the long stretch of highway that would last another four hours, when she broached a topic that had come up at the parent-only session.

"Some of the mothers were mad when they learned there was a women's clinic on campus," my mother told me from the driver's seat of the 1973 Ford Maverick she'd bought as a second family car. It was passed down through all three children and now passed back to her.

"Why would they be upset about that?" I asked, completely unaware of its significance.

"Because girls can get birth control there *without* their parents' permission," she said more matter-of-factly than I was used to hearing. "But I was thinking that they should be happy that their daughters will have a place to go for protection—just in case they need it."

I glanced at her, amazed she was using words like "birth control" in the same sentence as "daughter." While parents of my female friends and relatives had warned their girls to keep their legs closed or stay away from "fast" boys (the ones who talked fresh and had hands that liked to grab female body parts), I had never been cautioned about any such things from my own mother.

If she saw me looking at her, she didn't acknowledge it. Her eyes stayed focused on the multilane highway. I took the wrapper off my favorite candy—a Hershey bar, and commenced eating it, one chocolate square after the other. We sat side-by-side in our bucket seats, cars whizzing by at 55 mph, as if watching a movie with the *The End* popping on-screen before fading to black.

While she continued driving up the East Coast, the comfortable silence we had established over the past three years became our third companion. We were left to live as a twosome after

Katrina with her mom at her college graduation, 1984

my brother, the middle child, started his studies at Michigan State. My mother filled our mother-daughter time with Saturday trips to Burger King and her beloved pastimes—sitting at the kitchen table playing board or card games she'd taught us as youngsters.

It had not yet occurred to me that in a few weeks she would be repeating this same route, with only silence, intermingled with the sounds of radio disc jockeys and the instrumental tunes she favored, riding shotgun. Nor had I considered that for the first time in her life she would return to a home void of other people.

My mother was born in a house nestled on the west bank of the Hudson River thirty miles north of Manhattan in a town originally named Havestroo (meaning oat straw) by its Dutch settlers but was changed to Haverstraw in the late 1800s. Her North Carolina-born father moved there from the South during the Great Migration to work in the brickyards; her mother worked as a domestic. Before my mother was old enough to start school, her parents would move from what was once known as the "Brickmaking Capital of the World" to Harlem just around the onset of the Great Depression.

Her parents would later divorce and, at the age of nineteen, she would lose her thirty-nine-year-old mother prematurely to complications related to high blood pressure. My mother landed back in Haverstraw living with her mother's brother and his wife, right next door to the house where she'd been born. She had no way of knowing that she would bring all three of her children home from the hospital to live intergenerationally with her uncle and aunt until their death.

The summer I left for college, my mother was a fifty-four-year-old woman who had been made a widow by her estranged husband years before. Ebony, our loyal German shepherd, would be her only housemate.

A year later, I returned to Haverstraw for my first summer break. That summer I met the younger brother of a family friend visiting from South Carolina, and I began to spend most of my free time with him. On a typically hot day in June, my mom walked through the door and up the steps of our split-level house to find the two of us sitting together on the living room couch. She gave more than a glance but less than a stare at him perched on her plastic-covered orange and white floral sofa with his arm around my shoulder.

I gave quick introductions from my spot next to him before my mother walked into the kitchen to relieve herself of two armfuls of brown paper bags with the A&P logo imprinted on the sides. Perhaps it was the whispers and laughter she heard being exchanged over the sounds of cabinet doors opening and closing that set off alarms. Because as soon as she finished shelving the canned, bottled, and boxed goods, my mother was back at the entranceway to the living room.

"Trina, can I see you in my room?" From her tone I knew it was more a command than a question.

I got up and followed her down the hallway as dutiful as a soldier marching behind her five-foot-tall commanding officer, all the while wondering what could be so urgent.

"What's going on here?" she asked as soon as we entered the room and she shut the door behind us. Her words set the stage, converting her master bedroom with its crisp white walls and hardwood floors into an interrogation chamber.

"Nothing," I told her, unsure where she was going with this line of questioning.

"Why does he have his arm around you?" she continued to grill me.

The stance my mother took at that moment was a familiar one. It was the same one that she gave the white department store clerks who dared to usher her straight to the sales rack the moment she entered the store or follow her from aisle to aisle doing their worst imitation of a private detective. Like my favorite comic book superheroes, she would transform from being my mom into her fearless alter ego that used her intellect, dignity, and moral compass to take down those who tried to put anything over on her. She could and would make you feel as if you'd been put in your place without ever using a single profanity, which she never did. I've seen many a salesman and saleswoman apologize to her before she would leave the store and spend her money elsewhere. In those moments, she became my hero.

It was moments like those when I knew she didn't belong in small-town Haverstraw. She knew it, too. That's why she quit her job ironing handkerchiefs and enrolled in a four-year college in Salisbury, North Carolina, the year she turned twenty-three. After graduation she returned to Haverstraw, the only college-degreed black person of her generation residing in the suburban village or miles around it. But she soon found out that the 1950s integrated school district still wasn't handing out teaching jobs to qualified black women. She would accept a teaching position in North Carolina, but eventually family obligations would bring her back to her hometown, where she would live for the next thirty-two years, raising a family and teaching special education at a New York state residential psychiatric center.

As much as I admired my mother's intelligence and verbal proficiency, I questioned her decision to take us into an uncharted talk about romance, relationships, and whatever else she dared to bring up while we stood on opposite sides of her queen-sized bed that summer's day. I doubted she had the experience to steer me in the right direction. Although she had been married for fourteen years before she became a widow, she and her husband had lived many more years apart than together. Wedding portraits encased in silver frames or photos of any kind that showed my mother in the arms of a man had never existed as far as I knew.

"Are you serious?" I asked in a voice tinged with more sarcasm than I intended. "It's nothing," I tried to assure her. "All we are doing is sitting in the living room talking."

Mother wasn't buying what she thought I was trying to sell. But the more she pressed me about the relationship, the angrier I grew. Fueled by the accusations about my late-night whereabouts, I become increasingly agitated.

"We go to the movies and spend time at his sister's house," I told her in defense. "Besides, I can't believe you're questioning me about what I'm doing. I'm in college and you have no idea how I spend my time when I'm there."

"You're still living in my house," she reminded me.

Her words mimicked the ones my sister, brother, and I heard on Sunday mornings after late-night partying. My mother loved the Lord. She believed in Jesus—the Son of God, the savior, and the friend who will stick closer to you than a brother. She determined her children would, too. If you weren't suffering from menstrual cramps, running a fever, or recovering from surgery, then Sunday mornings were synonymous with church-going as long as you lived under her roof.

The house rules hadn't changed because I had lived in campus housing for a year. So it made no difference when my normally alto-pitched voice jumped octaves to protest, "I'm nineteen!"

I may have had problems controlling my tone, but my mother's never wavered when she responded, "I just hope you're not that desperate for love."

Taking into account the subject she approached on the car ride home from our parent-student orientation, coupled with her overreaction to a simple embrace, I suspected her concern was valid. A careless mistake on my part could alter my life's journey, or I'd wind up back in Haverstraw working at one of the state institutions.

But I chose to ignore the hint of fear I heard in her voice. I chuckled. "Desperate?" I tossed the word back at her. "I'm not desperate for love. I have a boyfriend at college. This is nothing for you to worry about."

My mother didn't appear to be convinced nor satisfied with my explanation, but with a shrug of her shoulders she dismissed me nonetheless. "I guess you and I are just two different people."

"Yes we are!" I concurred with as much indignation as I could muster. "Definitely! Completely different people," I added before stomping out of the room, half expecting her to chase after me, grab me by my arm, pull me back in the bedroom, and let me have it. My heroic mother, though three inches shorter than me, was more than capable of such an action.

Like the brief exchange about the outraged parents and the women's clinic a year before, my mother and I would never revisit the argument we had the summer of 1981. Instead, I would repack my four-piece, mustard-yellow, hard-covered American Tourister luggage—a high school graduation present from my mother— and prepare for the road trip back to Washington, D.C.

I moved into a new dorm a few weeks into August to begin my sophomore year at Howard University. My mother helped me unpack. We hugged before she, her best friend, and my broth- er took off in the direction of I-95 North. That was last time my mother would help me move into a dorm.

I never returned to Haverstraw to live, not even for a summer.

Something had shifted in the weeks leading up to my depar- ture as we wordlessly conceded that we are perhaps most alike in our individual need to embrace independence. My mother vol- untarily emptied her nest of her lastborn, choosing to entrust me to live my own mistakes and learn from the consequences. Her courage to set me free gave me the confidence to take flight and find my own inner hero, to embrace fearlessness balanced with faith-filled pursuit of my life's passions. I treasure this gift she gave to me and, like a priceless family heirloom, I'm making plans to pass it on—to the soon-to-fly-away daughter of my own—in hopes that she will soar even higher than those before her.

Motherless Child

Nancy LaTurner

*T*he tinny crackle of the communications radio blended into my dream and turned into crows squawking in a cornfield. Their strident caws metamorphosed into a human voice that dragged me upward to the surface of sleep.

"Eagle Twenty, Eagle Twenty, this is Eagle One, over."

I recognized the call signs. Eagle One, the Marine Security Guard at the embassy, was calling my husband, Fred.

When Fred was on duty, as he was in the earliest morning hours of February 14, 1983, he had to go to his office at the American Embassy in Mogadishu at any hour of the day or night to receive and distribute urgent cables from the State Department in Washington, D.C. The cables might concern government business, but too often the middle-of-the-night call-ins announced family emergencies for Americans employed by any of the many agencies working in Somalia.

I buried my head under the pillow while Fred murmured his acknowledgement into the two-way radio handset and fumbled for his jeans and t-shirt. As soon as he left the house, I went back to sleep. Or I thought I slept. I dreamed that I saw my mother standing in the doorway, backlit by the night-light in the hall. Or I thought I dreamed.

Two hours later, Fred laid his hand on my shoulder with gentle pressure. "I don't know how to tell you . . . the telegram . . . your mom passed away."

I knew it. My mind's eye held the image of my mother standing in the bedroom doorway, surrounded by a halo of pale yellow light.

Nothing had prepared me for the shock of my mother's sudden death. She hadn't been well, but her illness wasn't supposed to be fatal. She had tried many different kinds of treatments over the years—medical, homeopathic, herbal, as well as spiritual—but periodic blood-letting seemed to be the only therapy that helped. The name of her condition was polycythemia vera, an incurable DNA mutation that caused her bone marrow to produce too many red cells. The excess of red cells made her blood thick, caused her spleen to enlarge, and put her at great risk of stroke from clots. The hematologist told her

Nancy and Avis, her mother, 1942

that she could expect to live another twenty years if she continued to have regular phlebotomies to reduce blood volume.

Typical of Mom's way in the world, she didn't discuss her sickness with me or talk about the treatment or how she felt about it. She gave me the facts and nothing but the facts. Because everything seemed to be under control, I didn't worry or press her for details.

Dad told me later that Mom had had a good report from the doctor on Friday and she seemed happy and hopeful for the first time in years. On that Sunday morning he slept longer than usual and nudged Mom to tell her they were going to be late for church. Her body was already cold.

At forty-two, I was not ready to be a motherless child. Fred said that I handled the loss of my mother courageously, but I didn't feel brave inside. A strange numbness allowed me to go through the motions of my life, but savage screams of regret echoed in my head. I despaired the loss of any chance to say good-bye, any opportunity for Mom and me to make peace. Gaping holes riddled our relationship. Holes that I could no longer hope to fill or mend.

My brother in Minnesota and my father's three sisters in Florida flew to him in Los Lunas, New Mexico, right away. But

Dad begged me not to come. A winter storm had socked in the whole eastern seaboard and he worried that I would be stranded in New York, or worse. I agreed. I didn't feel capable of making the trip from Somalia to New Mexico in treacherous weather. Both my body and soul seemed as fragile as new ice, ready to shatter at the least pressure. I wanted to hunker down with my husband and our two children and pull the covers up over all our heads.

I made the right decision to stay in Somalia, I think, looking back, even though I had to grieve all over again when we went home for R&R that summer. I thanked God Dad had the loving support of family and church. At the same time, I ached with the pain of loss and loneliness, as I struggled alone to come to terms with my own emotions.

Of course, I expected to be sad. I didn't expect to be overcome with paroxysms so fierce they turned my body and my spirit into one wrenching spasm. I relived the overpowering contractions of childbirth as I suffered the agony of mother-death. But, unlike the birth experience, there was no gain in this pain, only loss. Grief overwhelmed me at odd moments. There was no logic in it. Waves of sadness ebbed and flowed in a tide that bore no relationship to my conscious thoughts. In the middle of a ladies' luncheon at the Ambassador's residence, I spoke about the batch of new educational videotapes donated to the school library, and the next second I was sobbing into my napkin.

When I thought about my mother, I regretted never telling her that I understood why mothering was a difficult role for her. She had been traumatized at the age of two when a stroke killed her own mother. Her only memory of that time was a horrific scene where she was held over the coffin in the parlor and forced to kiss her dead mother's cold, hard lips. From age two to eleven, she lived in an emotional limbo with her withdrawn father and stoic German maternal grandmother. When she was eleven, her father hired a housekeeper, a "widow" with a one-year-old daughter. Within a year, the housekeeper became Mom's stepmother and Mom lived her adolescence like Cinderella, chastised for leaving dust on light bulbs or forgetting to take the washing down from the clothesline.

I wished I had encouraged my mother to seek help for her depression. As a child I felt responsible for her moodiness, but try as I might, nothing I did made her happy. My childhood, indeed my whole life, was dedicated to being good, pleasing my mother, and taking responsibility for the happiness of everyone around me. I tried to be perfect, as if that could cure all ills. The burden of guilt over my mother's unhappiness warped my childhood, fueled my decision to study psychology, and spurred me into therapy in my college years. But I never discussed depression, mine nor hers, with my mother.

If we had ever had a heart-to-heart, I would have told Mom that I loved her. And I would have praised her intelligence and her accomplishments in business, art, and music. I might even have been courageous enough to show her how I learned to be a better mother from her shortcomings. But Mom was gone and I could only mourn her passing and the lost chances to mend our tattered relationship.

I tried running as an antidote, but when a breaker of grief rolled over me during a run, I stopped breathing. The effort of crying stole all the oxygen from my aerobic exercise and I fell to my knees with a frightening weakness as debilitating as an asthma attack.

Life went on, as it is known to do. Three months passed and brought us to R&R time. I looked forward to going home to see my dad even though I dreaded experiencing what home was like without Mom. I was relieved to see how Dad had coped with the loss of his life partner. He still lived with shock, disbelief, and overpowering sadness, but he lived. Mom and Dad had developed a very efficient division of labor during their forty-two years together, and Dad had much to learn about all the things that Mom had taken care of. She did all of the cooking, cleaning, grocery shopping, and bookkeeping. She was the one who remembered birthdays and anniversaries and kept photo albums up to date. At the time of Mom's death, Dad knew how to make a peanut butter sandwich, but he didn't know how to write a check.

Dad's three sisters had dealt with Mom's clothes and cosmetics, but Dad wanted me to sort out her papers, jewelry, and craft materials. I needed a box of tissues at my side during the many days it took to go through it all. Mom had never thrown away a single scrap of paper. I found cancelled checks from the 1940s, autograph books from her high school days. I cried over the poignant mixture of useless junk and precious treasure. Mom had no jewelry of any value beyond the sentimental, and I kept it all.

As I went through her extensive collection of craft materials, especially the fabrics, I had many moments of overwhelming nostalgia. Tears flowed and I plucked tissue after tissue to wipe, dab, and clench into a sodden ball.

I picked up a piece of yellow cotton with black scissors printed on it and remembered the oversized pincushion she made of that fabric to attach to her ironing board. She was a skilled seamstress and I learned many sewing techniques from her. I smoothed the bright yellow swatch on my knee and traced the stripe of scissors with my finger.

Oh, Mom, why didn't we understand each other? Was I such a difficult child for you to raise? I know I wasn't hyper, or sassy, or naughty, but was I too independent or precocious?

The red and white polka dots of a remnant from my childhood bedroom curtains caught my eye. Mom used that same fabric to line the shelves of my bookcase and to make a dust ruffle for my bed. I laid that polka-dotted piece across my other knee.

Why were you so sad? I tried to please you, but nothing I did made you happy. Nothing I did was ever good enough.

I pictured Mom standing in her kitchen surveying the tidiness and chrome sparkle with her hands in the wide front pocket of her favorite Kelly green apron. I stroked each tiny ladybug in the print on that scrap of fabric.

You taught me to be considerate of others, and I learned to put everyone else's happiness ahead of mine. But you still locked yourself in your room and cried for hours. You were broken and I couldn't fix you.

A piece of blue-and-white checked gingham triggered a vivid memory of Mom's square-dance dresses. She sewed circle-skirted outfits in every color with matching shirts for my dad so they could twirl away their Saturday nights in style.

I try so hard to be good! I epitomize the good child, excellent student, valued employee, loyal friend, virtuous wife, capable partner, and devoted mother. But I still feel unworthy.

Now that you're gone, I never will earn your approval, will I?

Compelled by a life-long creative urge, I concentrated on making something out of Mom's fabric scraps. I picked the pieces that held the best memories and sewed them into a quilted wall hanging. Buttons, lace trim, and embroidery embellished the simple rectangles of my design. The act of patching together the fragments of remembrance sparked the beginning of a healing process in my core. When I finished the quilt I had a tangible tapestry of Mom's life in primary hues.

The basic colors grounded me in the simple truths Mom lived by: "Do unto others as you would have them do unto you" and "Anything worth doing is worth doing well." I rubbed her silver fish charm sewn on the yellow panel and grasped the engraved words "It's Possible." As if Mom had whispered in my ear, I understood why she prized that charm. I've kept the patchwork with me ever since and it always hangs where I can see and touch it every day.

Mom's appearance in my dreams would have comforted me while I mourned, but I slept without dreaming. Every morning when I woke into the between time, I felt whole and complete until wakefulness prevailed and reopened an unfathomable void in my chest. I got up and walked my walk and talked my talk, but I was not entirely present in my life. It took me many more months to learn that the one real relief for grief is time.

A Moon Song

Barbara Toboni

I woke to the sounds of my mother in the kitchen. Her slippers scuffed the linoleum floor as she filled the teapot. My older sister, Nan, was still asleep in the twin bed next to mine. I tried not to wake her; I wanted some time alone with Mom before going to school.

She sat at the Formica table just a few steps away from the small kitchen. The dinette set, like the tweed couch and the television, came with our apartment. This was the second rental we had lived in since flying out from Philadelphia to join Dad. California was our home now; our family was together again.

Mom lit a cigarette. A haze of smoke hid the orange label on the Sanka jar. "Don't talk to me until I've had my coffee." Coffee and a cigarette—her morning ritual.

I waited—I knew better than to say anything yet. Finally, she stubbed the butt into the ashtray.

"How long will you be gone?" It was the same question I asked last week.

"Just a few days." A smile softened her face. She was beautiful to me, just sitting there at the table, no makeup, just my plain mom. I felt loneliness seep in. I didn't like sharing her with anyone, and I missed her when she was gone.

Just two years earlier, when I was five, my parents told Nan and me that Dad was going on a business trip, out to California, and that he'd be gone a long time. Dad packed his bags and left us in Pennsylvania. Years later they told us the trip was a lie, that they made it up because we wouldn't understand their separation.

Their separation lasted a year. That same year, 1959, Mom started her singing career and rehearsed most afternoons with her pianist,

Walt. Walt was a kind, middle-aged man who lived alone with his big orange cat. I adored the cat and Walt's cluttered house. Once I asked him if he intended to marry my mother. Surprised, he laughed, but it seemed like a reasonable idea to a little girl in need of a father.

Mom hired a live-in maid to take care of Nan and me while she worked nights. Delores walked me to school and made mayonnaise sandwiches just how I liked for lunch, without the baloney. She was surprised to find me one morning sitting alone on the front steps.

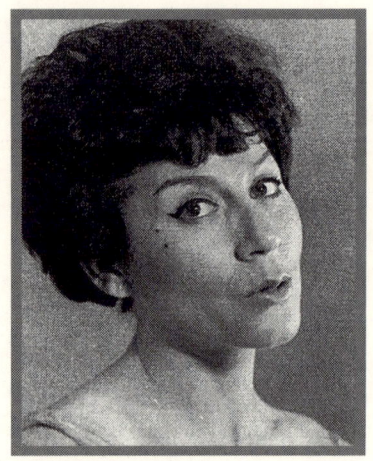

Irene Barri, 1964, when Barbara was 10 years old

"Barbara, why aren't you in school?"

"I want to be here when Dad comes back."

Dad wrote me letters about sunshine and swimming pools. He told me that he loved me and wanted all of us to come live with him one day soon.

I asked Mom how soon.

"We'll see, maybe for a visit," is all she said.

The year I turned six we flew out to Los Angeles. Dad handed us all sunglasses at the airport, and we went for a drive along the coast and ogled the Pacific Ocean at Huntington Beach.

Mom's eyes filled with tears. "It looks wonderful."

"I told you things would work out," he told her.

Dad opened the wrought iron gate to our first apartment building in Costa Mesa. My sister and I ran to the edge of the huge swimming pool, the pool that Dad described in his letters, and dipped our hands into the sparkling water.

That first rental was on the second floor. My sister and I shared a room with twin beds. When we caught the measles the beds became trampolines. My mother kept us indoors and brought home coloring books and crayons and a red rubber ball we bounced on the walls. The walls couldn't contain all the noise we made that day, giggles and creaking bedsprings, but Mom didn't complain. She made special allowances for her wild, itchy daughters.

A year later we moved to Orange. Our school was a long walk away. Behind our building was an orchard full of blossoming fruit. Nan held my hand as we passed beneath the rows of trees on our way to school. I was always tempted to steal oranges, but Nan, ever wary, yanked me away just in time.

Once, on our way home, it rained and there was nothing I could do but get wet. When I tramped in the door, Mom apologized, but there was nothing she could do either. She didn't know how to drive. Back East busses took us everywhere. In California, freeways sprawled for miles, and there were cars everywhere.

Mom was determined to learn how to drive a car. Dad took the whole family to the park and she drove around and around the block. My sister and I were proud of her. I didn't know then that she wanted to drive because she planned to continue her singing career; transportation would provide an opportunity for my mother to meet the right people and pursue her dream.

In the early sixties, Mom found work at the Purple Onion and the Hungry I, two nightclubs in San Francisco. Many celebrities got their start there, Bob Newhart and the Smothers Brothers. She sang cabaret and starred in *Annie Get Your Gun* and *Kiss Me Kate*. She could sing any song requested and she danced, too.

Nan and I helped her learn the lyrics to the song, "Triplets." The song, from the film *The Band Wagon*, had lyrics that were complicated but funny. We giggled our way through each verse.

From our apartment in Orange, Mom traveled to the airport in Los Angeles and from there caught a plane to San Francisco. Once in San Francisco she stayed at the home of friends, two male opera singers. One of them played piano so Mom could rehearse.

When she left L.A., Dad took us to the airport to say good-bye. We watched the big silver jet take off, and then Dad would take us somewhere, maybe to Thrifty for an ice cream or to the beach. I loved the beach, but the seagulls reminded me of Mom's airplane, the airplane that stole her, deposited her on stage somewhere to sing for strangers. Three nights and two days later, Mom flew home.

"Do you have to go?"

"Yes, honey. But you know what? You can help me practice, you and Nan, today after school."

My sister sat across from me at the Formica table, dressed and ready for the fourth grade. I wished there was some excuse to stay home, but I knew better than to pretend I was sick. I couldn't risk disappointing her if she found out I was lying. I shuffled off to get dressed.

After school we rehearsed. Mom sang the melody while Nan and I sang the chorus. Sometimes my sister got teary-eyed.

"Don't you think Mom's voice is pretty?"

I agreed. Mom's notes rang out rich with emotion. When the words were happy, her voice cheered. When the words were sad, her voice wept.

The singing was fun, but saying good-bye was hard. I hugged her tight, smelled her perfume, tried not to cry. The separations seemed easier for Nan than for me. My sister made friends easily, but I felt awkward around my classmates. Some of the kids teased me, said my East Coast accent sounded funny. I looked forward to spending time with Mom each afternoon.

Dad hired a neighbor to watch us after school. She taught us how to do chores. Dad was thrilled I was learning to keep house. He said Mom would be proud of me, how I was taking good care of the apartment and of him.

That was one of the points of our mother and daughter good-bye talks.

"Will you take good care of your father for me?"

"Sure, Mom. I can cook and clean. I know how to make tuna salad now."

"You can clean the house?" Mom seemed pleased.

I did everything to gain her approval. I sang with her. I piled books on her stomach to help her exercise her diaphragm. I wrote the lyrics to her songs in big letters so she could study them, but what I really wanted was to spend more afternoons with her. I loved our time together. I snuggled in bed next to her and brushed her hair or watched her eyes track each sentence as she read to me, her perfect voice lingering on each word. Other children looked forward to the weekend. I dreaded the days my mother was away.

Mom tried to reassure me. "You know we have a bond, a mother and daughter connection, don't you? I always know when something is wrong."

I nodded my head. Our bond was a holy thing. When we talked about it, we'd describe it as a long cord that connected us always, no matter what. That cord made me feel stronger about letting her go.

One night we peered out the balcony window. The shining moon pressed its face against the dark sky.

"You know, Barbara, when I'm away, I see the same moon. Before I go to sleep at night I pretend to see your face, so I can say good night. Can you see mine?"

I stared until my eyes blurred. "Yes. There you are."

The Civil Service hired my father and our family moved to Guam when I was thirteen. My mother continued her career, touring Japan, Singapore, and Australia. She was gone for weeks or months at a time. Our good-bye chats were more about writing letters and staying safe and less about my tears and letting go.

The moon continues to be a symbol for my mother, a way to stay connected. My family teases me when I'm in the mood for a chat with my mother, but I don't care.

"Hello, Mom," I'm known to say to the full moon. "I see you've come for a visit."

"Hello, Irene." My husband adds and my sons join in. We're all glad to see her.

Although it must have been hard for my mother to say good-bye to her girls, it was something she knew she must do. Certainly, the money brought comfort to our family, but singing gave my mother something more, the realization of her dream.

When I was young, I thought my mother sang because she wanted to become famous, like Barbara Streisand or Cher. Later she told me fame wasn't important. She enjoyed singing and wanted to share her happiness with others. She lit up when she talked about performing on stage, the places and the people she met, and their reactions to her talent.

Mom might not have known it at the time, but she was teaching me to make sacrifices for my own dreams. I loved caring for my first son when he was a baby. As he grew, I was determined that things would be different for him. My future could wait.

My child wouldn't feel lonely because I chose a career. A good mother cooked and cleaned and went for play dates to the park with other moms. She stayed close to home. My son wouldn't have to look at the moon to say good night.

But wasn't there more? I started to feel blue and didn't understand why.

In time, I remembered that I loved writing. I hired a baby-sitter once a week and took classes to sharpen my writing skills. When I started to share my stories and poems with others, it lit up my spirit. Writing was how I expressed myself; it was my song. Writing allowed me to open my heart and feel joy. My son had a better mother, a happier mother, just like my mother had been.

Mom died at the age of forty-eight, from ALS (Lou Gehrig's Disease). My father called me at work that day. I knew my mother was dying, but I didn't know it would be so soon. I couldn't be with her at the time because I lived in Guam and she had moved back to the States. Thankfully, my sister was by her side, caring for her.

I left work and went home. My husband and I were invited that evening to dinner at the home of friends. I didn't feel like going, but I pushed myself out the door, thinking it might be good for me to talk about what happened.

After our meal there was a knock at the door. Company had dropped by. A while later, another knock, and more company crowded into the small front room. It was an unexpected gift to be surrounded by so many friends who offered their sympathy. I will always believe my mother's spirit reached down and gathered everyone who cared around me.

Although it was a shock to have my mother struck with a fatal disease, I already knew how to say good-bye. Mom and I had practiced good-bye all our lives.

Edgewood

Clarice Stasz

*I*n 1945 my family moved from Indianapolis to Audubon, a small town in South Jersey, a short bird's flight across the Delaware River to Philadelphia. Our shingled bungalow sat on Edgewood Avenue, with sketchy remnants of a woods spread across the street. A larger spread, known as The Woods, covered what should have been four blocks next to the high school up the street.

Two years later, on my sixth birthday, my mother delivered a baby sister, and sixteen months after that, a brother. Little did I know, the worm that was to devour our family was beginning to turn, with no predator bird to snatch it away and save us. I soon learned to escape, and given my parents' curious lack of concern, I roamed about with no one asking where I had gone. I wandered about the local creeks and fields alone, hiked up and down the blocks of neighboring towns, where the larger houses suggested, to my naïve mind, happy families within.

The only place I avoided was The Woods. Once, a whiskery and wrinkled neighbor explained, the town land was all forest, the land of the *Unalachtigo*.

Here is what she told me:

To clear land for gardens and fields, the European settlers chopped down oaks and maples, switched their giant bull-ocks to heave and pull the stumps and roots away, and burned the remaining brush. Our Woods survived because of a curse made by the last Indian to live in the area. "Destroy these woods," he had said on his deathbed, "and your lands will turn dry as dust, poisonous of any living creature or plant. Your corn will wither, and your cows will give no milk. Your dogs will flee, and no song-birds will sing in praise of the sun's rising."

No one believed him, of course, but strange things happened when anyone went into The Woods. One family, the Griffins, farmed most of this area. Mr. Griffin was rabbit hunting one day and, without thinking, followed a hare into the thickets. He tripped on a snarl, and his rifle went off, shooting him in the leg so badly he was lucky they didn't cut it off. Despite further mishaps to trespassers, no one believed the curse.

Clarice's mother, age 27, at her second marriage, to Clarice's father.

The turning point was the fate of Evangeline Griffins. The local Wilson boy, who had moved to Philadelphia where he owned a shoe store, courted her. His smart-dressing ways lured Evangeline, who was tempted by his talk of the shops and restaurants and fancy clothes. She saw her mother's gnarled hands, calloused by the years of scrubbing, kneading bread, and carrying water, and thought of her own, still smooth and creamy.

The Griffins despaired. As a child, the Wilson boy was known to shoot at cats just for fun, and one day set a corn-crib afire—a bad seed. They forbade Evangeline to see him. But he was clever and set out to seduce her through romantic imagery. "I will come every full moon," he tempted her, "and screech like a barn owl below your window as a sign I have come." And that is what he did.

Thus Evangeline pined over her almanac, counting days to the full face of the moon. Each evening she would retire to her bedroom early, brushing her lustrous locks and pinching her lips to give them color. Upon hearing his owl call, she would crawl out her bedroom window and go with her lover to the barn.

As it turned out, the Wilson boy was engaged to the daughter of an emporium owner in Philadelphia. One day Evangeline was lunching with friends in that city, when she overheard a woman at the next table bragging about her fiancé. How inspiring that he would leave uncultured South Jersey to make his success in the larger world! Already he had expanded his shoe store business to add a shop in Germantown! As the happy woman described her love's honey-blond hair and green eyes, Evangeline knew she was speaking of her own lover.

Evangeline so despaired she feigned illness to rush home. There she dashed to her room, pulled the almanac from her desk drawer to look ahead for his next appearance. Only three days!

That Saturday she brushed her hair with special fury and pinched her cheeks until she almost bruised them. At midnight, she heard the screech of the owl. But she found no sign of her lover. Instead, she saw a barn owl, its ghostly flapping directing her toward The Woods. Thinking it was a messenger, she followed it up the creek bed, into the dark, accursed land.

The next day Mrs. Griffin found Evangeline's empty bed. Her footprints drew the family to the creek, thence into The Woods. Her parents were so fearful they sent their oldest boy to look for her. When he finally reappeared, he was struck dumb; he had to be slapped and given whiskey before he could speak. Then all he could say was, she was dead.

Finally, some neighbor men offered to fetch her body. Following the boy's directions, they found Evangeline lying in a small sunlit glen in the middle of The Woods. She had a beautiful smile on her face and seemed at peace. But when they went to lift her body on the carrying board, they were stunned to find her hands missing.

What did she die of? Where were her hands?

They never discerned. As for her hands, many years later the Wilson lad, by then a prosperous middle-aged man, was killed with his wife in the explosion of a steamboat boiler on the Delaware. While cleaning out his house, an heir found a golden box with mother-of-pearl inlay. It had a lock, for which no key could be found. But one sister insisted she must have it for her jewelry and took it to a locksmith to be opened. When he did so, within they found a pair of blue silk gloves containing the bones of two human hands. In time they were given a proper burial atop Evangeline's casket. People say the night of that burial the barn owls gave a furious fuss. And ever after that, the Griffins preserved The Woods and kept people away.

The story is not true, of course. There was no wise old neighbor woman passing on to me a story of the town. It is a story I wished I had heard, from the storyteller I long to have had in my past. Lacking such, I made the tale up to fill an ache that has persisted no matter the abundant joys sufficient to dampen it.

Here are the true stories:

One day a construction crew appeared in the stand across the street and sawed down the trees, where they erected five identical Monopoly board Cape Cod houses of imitation stone. In one moved a middle-aged couple with no children, only a glistening coal-black cocker spaniel named PeeWoe. Ethel, the wife, always dressed in colorful silks and was made up as if ready to lunch in the city, although she never went anywhere. She let me sit upstairs in the den and play her records of *South Pacific* while she gossiped below with my mother. With someone to do her housecleaning, she spent the days quietly drinking while waiting for her husband, Clark, crippled by polio, to limp home. Knowing nothing about alcoholism, I thought Ethel's slurred speech a sign of sophistication.

Clark's career as an accountant flourished, and the couple moved to a larger house in an upscale town that was hard for us to reach by bus. (Like many women in Audubon, my mother did not drive, because public transportation was so convenient.) These visits were special events, where Ethel would take us to restaurants.

Because my family never went to restaurants, these experiences were as exciting to me as my daughter's trips to Disneyland years later. The crystal, the cloth napkins, the ritual with the waiter, the opportunity to sit midst other women in hats, gloves in their laps, the requirement to behave one's self, all fulfilled a hunger for respectability, unobtainable within my family circle. Little wonder my mother, daughter of a Hungarian charwoman, preferred the company of this witty, inebriated woman who recognized her secret longings.

My mother was the eldest of five girls, reaching adolescence during the Depression. She left school to serve as a social secretary to wealthy women in elite Shaker Heights, Ohio. There she practiced her impeccable, clear handwriting, imbued by the nuns at her Hungarian-speaking Catholic grade school. Daily visits through the servants' entrance to the pristine, calm, and artful atmosphere of the ladies' private sitting rooms to write invitations became a terrible attraction. She even glanced noted people who came through the front doors. (Bob Hope would become a lifelong acquaintance, but that is another story.) Perhaps there she absorbed her love of opera and fine art, her spirited motive for philanthropy, but at what cost, knowing she could never cross the front thresholds?

Escape she did, stealing a sister's best clothes, to flee to Chicago where she sang on the radio and competed in dance contests. A photograph reveals her sylph slim figure in a clinging satin gown, the closest she would ever come to resembling the ladies of Shaker Heights. By age twenty-one she was married, widowed, single parent to a daughter, and back with the family she had fled in Cleveland. The horror of losing her husband while pregnant meant she feared intimacy, could never become affectionate with her family members, yet never ignored a stranger in need.

The second story concerns the remaining parcel of The Woods beside the high school. Although a dirt road offered a major short cut to the town swimming pool, no one used it. Midway stood a two-storied wooden house occupied by the only black residents of the community. My mother once said they were the descendants of slaves attached to The Mansion, the town's sole Colonial dwelling, and had been given the property from their master upon being freed.

My mother was a notorious confabulator, but this was doubtless true. Possible proof is in a map that depicts the proportion of the population by race in various areas of the country for the year 1820. Those areas fifty percent black or more are bright yellow and cluster in the states of Georgia and South Carolina. Yet a small golden blob afflicts South Jersey as well, a glowing reminder that the peculiar institution of slavery existed north of the Mason-Dixon Line. The Woods protected its hapless family from harassment, just as the arms of its tree canopy embraced my secret rooms and fantasies.

Growing up in ethnic Cleveland, where everyone had a somewhat pejorative moniker—Bohunk, Polack, Jungle Bunny, Kike—and lived in a segregated enclave, my mother saw little unusual in the situation. Prone to salty language, she frequently invoked similar caricatures as explanation of another's deplorable behavior. Yet when those barriers shredded in the Civil Rights era, my mother was among the first to go to the projects and schoolrooms in nearby Camden and even don dashiki to make the children more comfortable with her. We never understood how this stalwart Republican activist, who continued her prejudicial patter, danced in the forefront of the movement, defiant of local wisdom.

The last story of The Woods is of creation and rebirth. In her early years on Edgewood, my mother planted tulips and vegetables, and my father built a grape arbor like the frame of a room. Within a few years, it formed a natural tent to sit under during steamy August days. The backmost section was all lawn, large enough for tag and stickball games. One Mother's Day, the family danced around a white birch my father planted in the middle of the backyard. The beauty of its thin, snowy bark was a symbol of affection between my often-battling parents.

Yet as the worm fattened in my father's mind, my mother abandoned the yard. A woman of once car-stopping beauty, she neglected herself, would not bathe, and flaunted her body while resisting any hugs or kisses. (Male classmates stopped to visit me, no doubt to spy her breasts, covered only by a slip, beneath a see-through nylon blouse.) Her decline matched my father's growing eccentricity to let nature take over in the yard. First weeds, then bush and brush moved in. After several years, tree pods dropped by birds matured to dominate, their canopies cutting out the sun. The lower growths died, and the ground became clear. By the time my parents reached their sixties, they had a maintenance-free yard, noisy with squirrels and birds, where many trees provided natural cooling for the house during the humid summers.

What was taken to be sickness then, my father's refusal to have a manicured lawn and well-controlled gardens was, in retrospect, prescient, the wisdom of the madman. It never occurred to me that my mother, the gardener of her twenties, would feel oppressed by these changes. She retreated from home to political organizing and charity fundraising. Though I resented her neglect then, in adulthood I realized the need for her escape, her powerful drive to be acknowledged.

After Dad died, my mother's bizarre patterns retreated. For the first time in her life she flew abroad, traveling with a tiny carry-on, using thin sanitary pads to save washing her underwear. I know this because she died on the road. I received that tiny case, along with her address books, filled with hundreds she befriended on these journeys. Their stories of her generosity, from a woman who never praised her children for fear of spoiling, only stoked my lifelong envy of those not related to her by blood.

While going through remnants of our troubled relationship, I re-read one of the letters. She just had all the trees in the yard cut down, except for those guarding the house from summer sun. "I need to breathe," she said. "The squirrels are a pain in the neck." Each year she proudly sent me photographs of her latest flower plantings.

Only then did I understand how she had achieved what she seldom found in her life, a semblance of respectability, a longing so unrecognized by me. She had been like Evangeline, her silk-gloved lady's hands severed and lying in a casket, to be reunited with her body, only in widowhood.

Not My Mother's Child

Ana Manwaring

The sounds of my footfalls echoed in the cement stairwell. The smells of antiseptic cleaning solutions, urine, and illness permeated the air as I approached the surgery recovery wing. The atmosphere of the hospital stairwell transported me back to a time barely on the cusp of my memory:

I'm at the hospital with my daddy, my tiny hand secure in his big square one. I think I'm looking for my mother because she no longer lives at our house. I see myself playing in the laboratory, happy; I have forgotten about Mommy.

How do I tell my story without pity, rancor, or guilt? Dad and his beautiful, sad first wife, Marguerite, adopted me, but the marriage didn't last and they divorced in 1952. After the divorce and Dad's ugly custody battle to keep me, the Episcopal minister, my godfather, introduced us to the woman who would become my mother. I know Dad thought he'd found a perfect wife and mother for his little girl—me.

Marjorie was nothing like the violent drunk Marguerite had become. My father's second wife, "Mom," brought her eight-year-old natural daughter and her adopted two-year-old son to the union. We became an instant family in 1955 with three small kids—I was smack in the middle at five years old. We were going to be one loving unit, indivisible, all for one and one for all.

I continued the climb up the hospital stairwell; dragging up one stair slowly after the other, the closer I got to the sixth floor. Once again I was looking for my mother. It was a beautiful day, and I wanted to enjoy the sunshine more than I wanted to read Danielle Steele's *Passion's Promise* aloud to Mom, but I'd promised and duty called. Unemployed, I was expected to show up every day until she went home, a hospital stay of about six days, and this was the third. Mom suffered from a myriad of "female" disorders and, when I was about twenty-seven, my doctor father booked her into Ross Hospital for a hysterectomy, a relatively major operation. I felt sorry for my mother. None of us had turned out the way she'd planned and she suffered with medical problems. This wasn't her first surgery.

Ana's mother, Marge Manwaring, 87 years old

I reached her ward and paused in front of the heavy door to her private room. I really didn't want to go in—why should I? Whenever she hadn't wanted to deal with me, she'd shipped me off—to my room, to distant cousins for extended visits, to all-summer summer camps, and later to boarding school for the rest of the year. She pushed me away from the family as often as she could and made my life miserable when she couldn't. Throughout grade school, I started my day with one of her tricks. She forced me to eat scrambled eggs that had formed a thick yellow crust by warming in the oven for an hour while I got up and dressed. My siblings ate cold cereal with fresh fruit and milk. I still gag over dried-out eggs. I learned early to live quite happily away from the stress of my family and actively sought out opportunities to get away.

That day in the hospital I was resigned to putting up with my mother's sharp tongue—she'd find some fault with me, I was sure. That was our pattern. "Why can't you be like your sister?" was one of her favorite taunts. Her two children could do no wrong. When my brother snuck cookies from the cookie jar, I was always the culprit in her eyes—always the accused. In time it didn't matter what happened, or if I'd been a part, I automatically felt guilty.

Even my face betrayed me. And when I actually did commit the crime, I was spanked to the mantra, "We only punish you because we love you." I see myself like a cartoon character with a big question mark over my head.

My thought process, while standing outside her door, went something like: why would these visits to see Mom be any different? I'll spend the afternoon and my siblings will receive her blessings for being considerate, visiting children. I churned the bitter taste across my tongue.

I can't pinpoint when my mother began to discriminate against me, but I spent my childhood and youth convinced that she did not love me and was purposely mean to me. On the surface my parents treated my siblings and me equally, but inequities abounded. We each received our parent's largesse—"because we love you equally," Dad liked to say, an insinuation of the lesser status of the adopted children. To mitigate that problem, Dad adopted both of the other children, and Mom adopted me. The outward manifestation of fairness was king in my family.

I hesitated too long at Mom's door, cudgeled by unresolved hurts. Underneath the show of loving equity the Manwarings put on, lived another face, petty and insidious. Now, I look back and laugh about what I still remember, but in the 1970s, much remained raw. One story has stuck with me—silly on the surface, but I've thought about it so many times, it has codified to a symbol of our relationship. Anyway, I never got to see the Beatles, and I'm still mad.

In 1963 when the Beatles came on the scene I caught Beatle Mania. My sister, at sixteen, preferred the Beach Boys. Mom bought her the first Beatles album anyway and told me I couldn't buy my own because we'd have two in the house. The two of them sat in my sister's room after school with the door closed and played the album just loud enough that I recognized it was the Beatles, but not loud enough for me to enjoy it. Later, when the Beatles played at the Cow Palace, she agreed to let thirteen-year-old me go, but refused to take me to buy the ticket, or allow me to take a bus—and laughed. I hated her.

Mom even picked on my dog. "That terrible dog" she called Pepper and clapped her hands, chasing the poor little dachshund into a corner of the family room, while the other two dogs roamed the house.

I squared my shoulders, took a deep breath, prepared myself for the worst, and pushed into the hospital room. Growing up, I had withdrawn into my own world of books and daydreams— miserable and disenfranchised and sure I was going crazy because my family denied what I knew to be true. It was hard to shake off the old feelings, even as an adult with my own life. Both of our patterns of aggression, anger, action, and reaction had settled into our marrow.

"Quit holing up in your room. Come join the family," my father often said. I wondered why he wanted me to be subjected to my mother's criticism and my siblings' taunts. He didn't see how it was, how could he—gone all day at work and puttering in his garage woodshop at night. I puttered with him when I could and talked about my experience of my mother, but Dad wouldn't hear me.

"Dad, Mom blames me for everything."

"No one blames you for everything."

"Mom calls me Pitiful Pearl and says I can't do anything."

"You can be anything you want to be."

"Mom says I'm too fat and can't take ice-skating lessons. Can't I go—please?"

"It's your mother's decision."

"Mom hates me."

"Your mother loves you very much."

After all, I was given everything, Dad reminded me—a good home, good schools, good medical care, I met the best people, and had opportunities. I was one of the "lucky" children, not stuck with the family I was born into like most kids, but special—chosen!

"You were a Love Child," Mom said, and to prove how special I was she arranged piano lessons, ballet lessons, swim lessons, horseback riding lessons, books, bicycles, cars, even a house. I owed it to her, so here I was.

"Hi, Mom," I announced myself. She stared from the slightly elevated bed out the window at the sandstone cut in the hillside. She looked disheveled, pale and drawn—old. This scared me. I thought about how she loved the view from our first home as a family—a custom-built ranch-style house on a lot leveled from the side of a sandstone hill one valley east. It overlooked the Corte Madera Creek and Mt. Tamalpais. The builder had included floor to ceiling windows and sliding glass doors along much of the length of the house to take advantage of the magnificent view. I loved the view, too. An early memory is of Dad convincing me a little green man and his little fleet of green dump trucks came and took the mountain away when the fog streamed in and covered it. But I had often felt that I was on the outside of those sliding glass doors, separated from my family. And standing in Mom's hospital room felt like one of those moments.

"Oh, Ann," she said and shifted her head on the pillow to look at me. "You're here. I think I'm dying."

Dad told me that she had complained about an earache. No one believed her, as the surgery was nowhere near her ears.

"You're not dying, Mom. Dad says you're doing well, healing. Here, let me fix your hair." I picked up her hairbrush from the flower-choked tray table and attempted to fluff her matted curls.

"No one believes me. I'm dying."

The room was silent. I returned the brush to the table. There was nothing I could do with her wiry hair. In my childhood daydreams, my family trusted and respected me. My mother didn't call me "Pitiful Pearl," the untrustworthy, uncoordinated, incompetent girl who would "never be able to drive a car, let alone walk and chew gum." My brother and sister didn't call me "ugly pugsly." In fact, I didn't have a mother or siblings in my fantasies.

"I believe you," I said to be agreeable. "But I talked to Dad last night and he says you're mistaken—"

"—No! I'm dying. I . . . " Her clawlike hand darted between the bed rails, her long nails perfectly manicured, reminding me of bloody scissors, the scissors she used that time she wanted me to cut my too long fingernails when I was fourteen and I'd refused.

I'd chewed my nails from early childhood and had finally broken the habit—I had fingernails! She got Dad and together they pinned me down and clipped them back to the pads of my fingers.

To be fair, I fought back, pushing Mom's buttons all the time, especially as a teen. I didn't want a bad relationship with my mother, but by then I didn't know how to end the vicious cycle of antagonism and punishment. I began to think of myself as the girl she accused me of being.

She gripped my wrist, "I was always jealous, you know. I hated that you knew your father before I did. I punished you for it. I treated you differently than my own kids—and I denied it. I'm sorry. I love you, Ann. I'm dying; can you forgive me?"

We clutched each other's hands and wept. I was vindicated. I'd yearned for this, to have a mother who cared for me, but would this change my life? Would she remember after she healed? Would I be able to change my way of behaving with her after almost a quarter century of calling her Mom? I didn't know, but I did know I was going to have to work at forgiveness.

Mom did have an ear infection, she did heal, and over the years our relationship grew and deepened. After Dad died, we formed a friendship, and I thought our past had healed too. I felt released; after fifty years, I didn't need to strive for her love anymore. I finally found my mother.

But Alzheimer's disease has played a dirty trick on us. On Christmas Eve, my mother asked, "Are you one of my children?"

Yes, Mom, I'm your daughter.

Little Traveler

Laura McHale Holland

I can recall several scenes from the two years when my mother's life intersected with mine. They are like pencil sketches drawn in haste on napkins and stuffed into pockets, not exquisitely rendered oil paintings on canvas hung with care on museum walls.

In one memory, my sister Mary Ruth comes to my crib. Her wide, blue eyes are the only part of the memory with color; most of the scene resembles the black-and-white television shows of 1950s America, which is the era of my early childhood. Mary Ruth calls out, "Mommy, Mommy, can Laura play?" At first our mother says no from another room, but Mary Ruth persists, wears her down. And finally my mother comes into the room. She has wavy, dark hair, glasses, and a gentle but distracted touch. She lifts me from my crib and, with a weary sigh, plunks me on the floor and speeds away. I begin to play with Mary Ruth and my other sister, Kathy, but I cannot keep up with them, which frustrates me. I begin to wail. My mother rushes into the room, picks me up, puts me back in my crib and leaves the room again.

I believe this sort of thing happened quite a bit and that I spent more time in my crib as a baby and toddler than is customary, but this is just my surmising. I cannot honestly attest to what day-to-day life was like for me when my mother was alive.

Another scene from that time takes place at my grandmother's apartment. My mother and father are standing at a window. They are facing each other, talking. She is dressed hat-to-shoes in pink, and I think she is as beautiful as a princess. My father notices me approaching and tells me to go away. "Your mother is on her way to church," he adds. My mother doesn't speak to me. She doesn't even turn her head to acknowledge my presence.

In the third memory that comes to mind, my mother puts me down on the floor in a neighbor's basement recreation room where a party of neighborhood children is in full swing. Laughter and chaos reign as she steps away from me and pauses at the bottom of the stairs to talk with another adult. I watch her at first, but then another child draws me into chasing a red ball or balloon. When I look over to the staircase a few minutes later, she is gone.

The fourth memory is different. It plays in my mind from three perspectives: my mother's, mine as a toddler, and mine as an adult. This multidimensional aspect of the memory both intrigues and unsettles me. I can reasonably assume the adult point of view is my imagination at work. But I'm not sure about my mother's point of view. Could I have experienced it as it happened from both my own and my mother's points of view? Author and educator Susan Cheever wrote, "There is no other closeness in human life like the closeness between a mother and her child. Chronologically, physically and spiritually, they are just a few heartbeats away from being the same person." But how close are mothers and their children, really, in those early months and years? How close was I to my mother? Can a mother and child experience one another's feelings and visions? Are we all born a little bit psychic and never hone our skills, so our nascent abilities atrophy like unused limbs?

These are questions I can pose but cannot answer as I reflect on this fourth scene. My mother and I are straddling the threshold of our front door on Tallman Avenue on Chicago's South Side. I am outside, my baby shoes scuffing on cement; she is inside, her leather pumps poised on wood. The day is warm, inviting and as calm as can be, given the hum of industry and traffic that envelops our days. I am small, very small, still in diapers, but big enough to follow my sisters, who have already scurried down our front walk and are calling to neighborhood friends in the high-pitched tones of children at play everywhere. The house is dark inside and cozy; the windows are dressed with white lace curtains, so sun dances through the holes and dapples the dark wooden furniture that is polished to a high gloss.

My mother has her hands on me and is loosening her grip,

letting me go, something she does as a matter of course. And I think nothing of this. On this warm day, I'm eager to get out and explore. She wears a silky, flowing dress. It's dark blue with a pattern of small, white flowers and little white buttons down the front. She doesn't say anything to me as I take one little step then another, moving across the porch to the stairs. I waddle down the stairs and onto the walk. I look out at the sunny scene, smell the air, which is pregnant with the scent of all the neighborhood's roses and lilacs and gardenias mixing in the humid air, and I am filled with wonder. Life for me in this moment is like a fairy tale when the good witch comes and everything sparkles with possibility, and your cares fade, and fairies are scattering their magic dust everywhere, making even the blades of grass and ants building their dirt hills hyper real, and nothing could be better than the present moment. There is no past or future. And this is how life is for me, I believe. I am either in my crib, bored, or I am out in this world of magic and wonder, mesmerized by it, trying to mesh with it and not succeeding, but not giving up either.

As I step farther down the path, I am moving with ease on my sturdy little legs. It's like time is suspended, and the world is in slow motion. I do not look back at my mother. It isn't a purposeful thing. It just doesn't occur to me to look back or say good-bye. I notice a light yellow butterfly flitting along some flowers to my right. The flowers are butter yellow, too. I stretch out my pudgy fingers, trying to touch the butterfly, and I am awed by the way it darts up and over. And then I hear my sisters, who have rounded a hedge and are now out of sight. They are calling to me to hurry along. And there, my young point of view stops.

Briefly, I see the scene as my adult self, but disembodied. I'm hovering at the sidewalk looking at my toddler self who is enthralled with the butterfly and flowers, which are now bobbing in a warm breeze. And then I look down the front path, up the stairs and I see my mother. She has closed the screen door but is still at the threshold, watching her youngest child.

Then my point of view shifts again, and I am seeing the scene from my mother's eyes. I am somehow both my mother and my adult self, fused into one. Our fingertips are touching the metal screen, our heart is pounding. We are watching the child stretch to reach the butterfly, and we say in a voice not loud enough for the child to hear, "Good-bye, little traveler." Sorrow then flows from my mother's body and fills the entire house. And I am suddenly disembodied again, but this time hovering behind my mother who lingers at the door but is now growing cold and hard, like one of those folk tale characters turned to stone for doing something stupid. I cannot fuse with her again nor can I do anything to help her. And when I, the woman I am now, recount this scene to someone, my voice cracks when I say, "Good-bye, little traveler." And I weep.

There is no face-to-face interaction between my mother and me in this memory. None of my memories of her contain that type of interaction. I don't remember her loving me. I only recall her spurning me, as in the day when she was all dressed up for church. I heard later that she had been sent away to "rest" at a medical facility in Wisconsin. She had been released shortly before the day I saw her talking with my father, but she wasn't yet ready to resume caring for my sisters and me. Sometime later, it could have been days or weeks, she felt well enough to bring us home from our grandmother's. But she stayed in the car parked at the curb while my aunt, her sister, came upstairs to fetch us. When we got down to the car, my mother was sitting in the front passenger seat and staring straight ahead. I threw a tantrum on the sidewalk and refused to let go of my grandmother's hand, until my exasperated aunt reprimanded me and settled me into the back seat beside my sisters. My mother was motionless and mute the entire time. I remember well the mix of anger, confusion, shame, and dread I felt as the car pulled away from the curb, but I recall nothing of the drive itself or arriving home.

Logically, I know my mother must have looked at me directly and spoken to me countless times. I have a snapshot of her holding me in her arms when I'm a baby, and she's smiling down at me—a full smile that lights up her face, nothing held back. But my memories reflect none of this. Barbara Kingsolver wrote that memory is "a complicated thing, a relative of truth, but not its twin." I do not know how closely related my memories are to truth; they are just little snippets with no real beginning or end. I only know that they are based on real experience.

I now suspect I am blocking out long-ago moments of motherly love and affection I must have experienced because it is more painful to miss someone who brought me into the world and loved me dearly than it is to be indifferent to the mother who spurned me while she was alive and didn't care enough to stick around and raise me. The truth is, I suspect, that she was both a loving mother who cherished me and a cold, despondent mother who killed herself to get away from a life she couldn't tolerate. A life that included me.

My memory of her body hanging from a basement beam is the point where her life no longer intersects with mine, although, as a two-year-old, I didn't know it at the time. It is the point where her death gets under my skin and, in subtle ways, constrains every breath I take to this day. But the memory of her watching me walk down our front walk at least entails her saying good-bye to me, even if I can't, and probably never will be able to see her bid me a fond farewell as my little self in her arms, looking into her eyes.

I think it is unlikely that she actually said good-bye to me directly. I wouldn't have understood the finality of such a farewell anyway, and she must have known that. Seeing her do it from a distance is probably the closest I'll ever come to her acknowledging that my time with her was coming to an end.

The messages my mother conveyed to me by destroying herself are far from inspiring. Among them are: help is not at hand, things will never get better, it's acceptable to give up in the face of extreme difficulty, and life is not worth living if you feel hopeless. Even more pernicious is the belief that love is not strong enough to drive demons from your door, demons that occupy a toxic pit inches from my feet, a pit that I fell into as a teenager and had to crawl out of inch by inch, year by year.

Eventually I learned that those demons, while always present, have no power over me unless I give it to them. It has now been decades since they've had a foothold in my life, and whatever their roots, my mother's demons have come to their end here with me. When my daughter was in middle school, one of her assignments was to sum up what she'd learned from her mother. She said I had taught her that life is a gift and you should enjoy each and every day. I was stunned. I had never said this to her. I was focused on messages like always do your best and you can do anything you put your mind to. But my daughter dug deeper and found wisdom I demonstrated in my daily actions but was not consciously aware of, wisdom that was hard-earned and far more important than any thoughts I may have about achievement. And what better message could I, a daughter of suicide, give my own daughter and the generations of daughters and sons who may follow?

The sorrow fused with my mother's choice to end her life when mine had barely begun still resides deep within me, a silent companion. But her legacy is nevertheless rich, not in the few facts my mother-memories contain, but in the way her actions forced me to live with darkness and find joy in life anyway.

Three Mothers

Deborah Jones-Norberto

*I*t is silent in the house. Warm sunlight floods in my bedroom window as I look out on the icy cold woods below. My children are still asleep and know only stories of my journey to motherhood. I know the reality. I have three mothers. One, chosen in grief, another lost to death, and one who created my body. I mother my children with no guidance, no hand to gently brush aside my hair and say, "You're doing okay." I am motherless and yet have three mothers.

I've tried to imagine how it must have felt to my birth mother to find out she was carrying a child she knew she couldn't raise. The moment I found out about my firstborn, a son, I was captivated. I knew I would never be able to turn away this child or the two daughters who followed him. Yet, even so, I was a child given up. I always knew about my adoption and made to feel privileged to have been "chosen." Never once did my adopted family make me feel like an outsider. I was joined to them eternally the moment I was taken in.

Although joyous for them, I can almost feel the emptiness that must have engulfed my young birth mother. She surely must have felt fear, given the uncertainty of the time period and the pressure from her parents to keep it quiet. I was told she was a college graduate who was to move abroad and become a linguist. My father was a supposed writer living in Greenwich Village at the time of my birth. After a lifetime of engendering that idea, I found out in my forties that my father was a wild, alcoholic Navy man, a man who fathered nine children with five wives. My mother was the daughter of a WASPy upper middle class, upstate New York family. They parted quickly and my birth and subsequent adoption were swept under the rug. She gave me my hair and eye color. She gave me my tenacity and focus. I inherited numerous traits from her and yet I cannot find her. She is truly a mystery to me and perhaps wishes it would remain so.

Jane, my adopted mother, left me too soon. She passed gently into death at age forty-five, when I was thirteen. Her ravaged body was so ill, so delicate from a lifetime of diabetes and heart disease. Her eyes could no longer see; so I was raised in a fascinating household of Braille and white canes. The ballet bars that lined the walls to help her balance became my dance bars. We would tease and laugh with games of hiding things, which she would always find. I watched her walk into walls, lose control of her bowels, and lapse into diabetic comas, all before I was eight years old.

Jane and Deborah, back porch, 1975

I have a vivid memory of getting ready for school one morning. It was a special day because I could wear my Campfire Girl outfit to school. I put on my navy skirt and crisp white blouse. I had a natty scarf with a little red pin in the form of bird on it. I still have that pin in my jewelry box. Unexpectedly, I heard my father shout to me, "Call the ambulance!" I ran into their bedroom to find Jane sprawled on the floor between the bed and the wall, my father frantically leaning over her. As realization struck, I ran to the kitchen, found the number pinned to the side of the phone, dialed it, and summoned the EMTs. I'm told I was brave and helpful at the time. All I remember is the fear of seeing my mother on the floor, the scramble of footsteps in my house, the surreal nature of her being carried down the stairs and into the ambulance. I ended up in school that day, still in my uniform. When I returned, I had no mother to hug me, no warm conversation to fill my afternoon, no one to tell me she was proud of me. I suddenly felt foolish to be in my Campfire Girl outfit on such a horrible day.

Through the ensuing years, many ambulances would be called; EMTs and day nurses became a part of my childhood. Shots of insulin in the morning would be given to her as I lay next to her in bed talking about the day ahead. I learned to test her urine, cook a pot roast, do her hair, pick up lost stitches from her knitting, and correct her typed letters. I was told that I was so mature, helpful, gifted. I only wanted a normal life and yet this was my "normal."

In her younger years Jane was a gifted teacher and librarian. I'm told her kindness and hospitality were endless. Even throughout her illness, we had parties and dinners. China and cloth napkins, two forks on the left, and lavish menus were normal for us. In her weakness, she was strong. She gave me the amazing gift of survival no matter what the odds. I learned strength through her dignified life. She gave me unconditional love, as her own mother gave her. They would talk on the phone with each other every night before bedtime. They were the best of friends. I want to be that mom. I want to talk to my kids and, more importantly, have them want to talk to me. So far, I've succeeded; my teens talk to me and my nearly tween is starting. It is a blessing.

Every year I visit Jane at her cold, lonely gravesite in Pennsylvania. I plant flowers and bring balloons as if she can see them. My children go with me. They are woven into my grief. My oldest daughter and I share the same age difference as my mother and I once did. She and I have an unspoken bond that is almost otherworldly. I gave her my mother's name as her middle name. We joke that my mother is coming back through her when she does something that I did years ago to annoy Jane. I believe that her spirit embodies my daughter, at times gently brushes my hair aside and tells me, "You're doing okay."

You would think the memories of my adopted mother and my lost birth mother would be the most painful ones, and yet it is the third mother who pains me the most to discuss. My stepmother came abruptly into my life one short year after Jane died.

I didn't want her. She most certainly didn't want me. She already had two daughters who, ironically, she had adopted also. My father was smitten and so we blended families to total six children. Three boys, three girls, a regular "Brady Bunch." Yet for me, it became a hellish, turbulent time in my life. The competition between a daughter and her new stepmother is no secret. They both vie for the father's affections and demand equality. Much to my dismay, I lost the conquest. I lost both my mother and father in the same year, one to death, and one to love.

I didn't really know it at the time, but my stepmother played favorites, even within her original family. She spoke with such assurance, never phrasing things like, "I imagine you're feeling bad," but with superiority and certainty, "You are feeling bad." She learned to control and guide people where she wanted them to go. My life prior had been honest and straightforward with my mother. We yelled at each other and then hugged and made up. This new life was different. My stepmother never raised her voice, but would softly call me "scum" and tell me how I had "displeased the family" when I stayed out too late or rebelled. I have painful memories of being balled into the fetal position behind my bedroom door while she "disciplined me," softly reciting my list of wrongs.

It eroded my self-esteem and ripped at my heart to see how my father had been duped into marriage with someone so cruel. She never did these things to her daughters and I put up walls to hide my feelings because of it. It drove me into an early, short-lived marriage with a man ten years my senior, just to get out of the house.

I imagined I would one day write a book entitled *Doorway to Hell* to describe the sheer terror of their bedroom door. They kept a combination lock on the door to keep us out. When I had to go in to be disciplined, I always came out broken—never physically, but always emotionally. At the time, my father seemed unreachable. He was still lost in grief and yet floating in his new love. He didn't try much to save me. He would work in the garage on some project or lock himself away in the unreachable bedroom. I jumped from one boyfriend to the next in an effort to feel the love that was lost.

Finally, my memories of Jane and the love she gave sustained me. It is the same love I've bestowed upon my own children. It is a love that has helped me to forgive my stepmother in my adult years. She has and continues to care for my father. She has apologized in her own way through gestures of kindness and love for my children. I've found that in forgiveness there is freedom and lightness of heart. I wanted my children to have a grandmother, unburdened by my past. I was willing to step out of the darkness and give them that.

I watch my children now. They are vastly different from each other but carry traits of myself in each of them. I see their struggles and their strengths. I see them draw from their own inner reserves much as I do and I think of my own journey to this point.

Three mothers—I was given up by one unable to keep me; embraced, yet left by one who couldn't stay; tortured and yet strengthened by one whose limitations didn't allow her to love me fully.

I know we are all woven into the fine fabric of our lives; my children are the threads that join my childhood with my adulthood. I imagine them as part of an intricate tapestry, a never-ending work of beauty and strength. I think on this quiet morning that my children will carry on my life and hope they find guidance, fulfillment, and love from others, but mostly from within themselves.

The Birds of Promise: A Letter to my Godmother

Tiah Marie Beautement

Dark clouds bearing evil intentions cloak our family tree. Their whispers draw us into a complex sadness, which we must fight, or we find ourselves banished into never-ending paranoia and grief. Yet, somehow, I have not succumbed. There have been periods of gray paired with too many tears. But even during that dark February hour of my senior year of high school, 1996, your hand extended, beckoning me to Houston, where the sun still shone, a marked contrast to the Oregonian winter gloom.

You were determined to soak me in Vitamin D. Off we marched through popular bird-watching trails. Handing over spare binoculars, you pestered me to notice the varied tips of wings and color of clawed feet. Of course, your bird book would usually announce that what I described did not actually exist. Such outings did not endear me to your feathered friends. I far preferred the living, breathing alligators, which were frequently seen leaning against the signposts cautioning walkers to give the beasts a minimum berth of thirty feet.

You were one of the few who did not pester me with questions about my future studies. Instead, we chatted politics over heaping plates of Tex-Mex. Or we reveled in the memories of the previous summer, when we rumbled down the West Coast Amtrak line to explore California universities. You were pleased with my final choice of school. Assured me that in time, the finer details would fall into place.

You were full of surprises that visit. Never one to follow fashion trends, you whisked me off to your hairdresser who sculpted my locks into a current look. Then we paraded my trendy do at a fancy mall, where racks of dresses stretched out farther than my hometown's grocery store.

I cautiously approached a group of cheaper dresses. You, in your tidy but plain polo shirt, plunged into the far more expensive displays. "Try this one," you said, holding up a long white prom gown.

I did. A perfect fit.

"Come out. I need to see."

So I did. A few women stopped. Admired. "Are you getting it?" one inquired.

"She is if she likes it," you grinned over my protests.

"You have a beautiful daughter," a woman said.

Ann Carleton (godmother), Tara Peakes (author's sister), Tiah Beautement (right)

"Goddaughter," you said. "And she is."

You made me drive us back to your home on the mind-boggling freeways. I'd never negotiated traffic of such proportions. "The traffic is just as bad in the Bay Area," you said.

Almost home, you had me pull over for gas, forcing me out to "fill 'er up"—something I had never done, since self-service remains illegal in Oregon. "You'll be having to do this, too, come September," you said.

The outing was very you—practicality blended with generosity and fun. A woman who controlled her life with detailed precision: weighed her ground beef and froze it into perfect portions, accounted for every cent, and used an item until it crumbled. Thus your pennies grew into dollars of comfort, portioned off into slices with which to support and often spoil those you loved. With tactful words, here and there, you guided me into understanding how to apportion my meager wages from summer jobs so that I'd be able to afford my books and still have a bit for fun.

It may have seemed odd to others that I was sent to you during my February blues. But my mother loved you. Do all sisters-in-law love so deeply? If the untimely demise of my parents occurred, my three younger siblings and I were to be your inheritance. Few could comprehend how a childless woman, single and free, could possibly be the obvious choice. But my mother knew. You were her only choice.

Our small town upbringing concerned you, educationally and culturally. As a self-professed globetrotter, you were desperate to make us understand that varied perspectives, customs, and, later, employment opportunities existed in the great beyond. You dragged me to Houston museums with dinosaur skeletons more than two stories high, to various city libraries whose children's sections alone dwarfed our local hub, and innumerable cultural events. You even arranged a week to explore Washington, D.C.

Could you feel me watching you? You made me practice riding escalators and elevators and taught me how to negotiate a revolving door. I observed everything and often copied. You slept without a pillow. After my unaccompanied visit to you at seven, I insisted on doing the same for almost twenty years.

Yet not everyone was full of admiration. You were often held up to my sister and me as a cautionary tale of women who waited too late. Our little ears picked up on the grown-ups' whispers and the subtle, and not so subtle, messages in books, movies, and magazines. A childless spinster was not on a par with a dashing bachelor. This state of singularity was an adult woman's worse sin, unless called to be a nun.

My mother was one of your most valiant defenders. "Your aunt is one of the most intelligent women I know," she often said. She sang your praises: a woman who had put herself through university, traveled the globe, lived and worked in both Honduras and Germany, then put herself through law school.

By senior year these whispers had grown louder and had widened to include me. My apparent lack of dating life became a Thanksgiving dinner topic amidst groans that I would end up like you. But that February I watched men watching you. While your hair was clipped short and your outfits were far from flashy, your confidence gave you poise that turned more than a few heads. When we socialized with your male peers, you shared well-considered opinions on current affairs, laced with humor and wit. I saw the men's eyes full of admiration and respect. It was on this visit that I realized then that your single life was not necessarily an accident, but a choice.

Such knowledge gave me confidence that, while I might choose someday to marry, there was nothing wrong with a life in which a woman owned her own home and her own car and was financially free to buy plane tickets as she desired. Fresh from this nugget of wisdom, I turned down every prom invitation and instead went with a group of friends. Clad in that long white dress, I was happily single and had an unforgettable night.

Then February returned. With one semester completed at college, I was back in Houston bearing a busted shoulder and no assurance it would ever fully heal. To boost my spirits you took me to Galveston Island so I could wander the streets, alight with Mardi Gras festivities. But of course there was a catch. Before we could collect beads and gawk at the flamboyant costumes, we had to hunt down your feathered friends, whose varied migration patterns intersected at the island. You confessed this was your favorite place in the world and I watched your eyes shine as the ferry carted us to and fro.

"Why not move here?" I asked.

"Expensive," you said.

Hard to argue, when I knew I was part of your expense.

The expense of me nagged. Before boarding the plane to California, I said, "I don't know if I'll ever be able to pay you back for all you've done."

"You will," you smiled.

I frowned, unconvinced.

A hug. "Don't forget me when I'm old. There is more than one way to pay a debt."

College expenses were overwhelming. My university encouraged students to undertake international adventures during the

January cram term. But the costs were far beyond my means. Even with student jobs, scholarships, and help, the debt continued to climb and, much to my chagrin, I doubted I'd ever have cause for a passport. But in the fall of my junior year, a full semester of South Africa was offered at an affordable rate.

"Do it," my mother said.

"Listen to your mother," you said.

I went, single and happy to be so, and then promptly fell in love. I left, only to return six months later. It was a choice, not an act of desperation. Thus I graduated in South Africa, complete with a fiancé and a load of student and emotional debt.

"You'll pay it back," you said.

Of course I would. I had promised. But how long would it take?

"There is time. Just remember me when I am old."

And so I went to England. Married. Saw Ireland, Italy, Germany, Switzerland, and France. "See Spain," you said. "It was my favorite." So I booked the tickets but missed the flight. "There's still time," you said.

During all of this emerged a dream that one day my husband and I would go back to South Africa. You made it clear that chilly England was out. So we talked about the houses in South Africa that came with their own granny flats. We compared numbers: food, clothing, rent, and health care. But most of all, I told you about the birds, in all their variety. You sounded enthusiastic. But perhaps you thought it was all a lie. Nor did you ever make that often-discussed visit to Europe.

February 2003 came with much unexpected news. I was alone in my one-bedroom flat when my phone rang. My maternal grandmother had passed. I was still clutching the receiver, tears streaming down my cheeks, when my husband burst in to happily announce he had been offered a new job, complete with an eleven-month stint in Chicago. Better fortunes were in store, but for now there was no money for an international plane ticket.

It is very strange to mourn alone. Nobody leaves breakfast on your doorstep. Nobody knows about the person you have lost. A spouse, a friend, all try to be sensitive to the pain, but you grieve in solitude while you carry on. With no funeral to attend, there is nothing to give pause to the mundane details of the every day. Then the final sucker punch, a Valentine's card, arriving on that very day, bearing a message from the dead: Sorry, this is late. *Love, Grandma.*

Once again, you reached out to me in the February gloom. You must have written to me the day after she died. Your letter provided the comfort and strength necessary to wade through the muck. You knew my grief. All of it. Completely. You had been there, too.

But I never knew your pain. Over the next few months in England, I wrote without receiving reply. When I phoned, you kept the calls abruptly short. When at last my husband's new company moved us to Chicago, May 2003, my invitations to meet up were dodged. Should I have guessed? Then again, these quiet periods had occurred before, and our communication had always resumed. I trusted you would make contact when time allowed, and I continued to write.

Mid-June 2003 my husband I went backpacking in Michigan. On my return, I wrote my final letter to you. It was never sent. While I had tromped through the Michigan wilderness, eaten by mosquitoes and investigated by curious bears, you were battling your own baying beasts. Running from their teeth, you fled to Galveston Island. With one last walk into the woods, you left us. Three shots to the heart. So precise.

My brain appreciates that this was not a choice as choices are understood to be choices. My own tiny tastes of these dark, murky clouds provide a sense of understanding that this sort of sadness is not one that can be brushed away with soft tissues and hugs. This is a monster that lurks in shadows that others cannot see, wrapping finely cut tendrils around its victim's soul, pulling harder and harder with each new dark day.

But it still hurts. Time does not heal; I merely grow accustomed to living with the pain. The questions will always remain barbed riddles with no peace. A woman so strong, so intelligent, so admired, a woman instrumental in the enrichment of so many lives . . . and you are missing it. The fruits of your labor, the goals achieved, the promises that would have been kept—if only there had been more hope. You were loved. And that love remains.

Your birds go on singing. They refuse to be ignored. Our home is near the nesting grounds of the rare oystercatchers. Your great-niece and great-nephew wake in the wee hours of the South African morning to the sound of the guinea fowl pounding on the sliding doors. The francolins trot out their chicks to peck as the children eat their own breakfast. Owls perch on the roof, scouting for prey as bedtime stories are read. During the day, I write at home, taking coffee breaks on the porch, and cannot help but see the sunbirds flit from branch to branch. Each spring we watch as the sugarbirds' tails grow into elaborate trailing ribbons. How I wish you were there the day I witnessed a small bird, in flight, desperately dodge an African Eagle's aerial attack.

But you missed it.

All because of your choice that was not a choice.

Tell me: were the birds with you when you died?

About the Contributing Authors

Tiah Marie Beautement is the author of the novel *Moons Don't Go to Venus*. Shorter works have appeared in Lit-Net, *Botsotso, Wordsetc, New Contrast, Flashquake,* and *Motherverse.* She is a born and raised Oregonian, living in South Africa after obtaining dual citizenship in Britain. No matter where she goes, people claim she talks funny.

EMAIL: tiah.beautement@googlemail.com

Danielle Christopher is a work-at-home mom of two young daughters. Her writing has appeared in *Women's Post* and *Hybrid Mom,* as well as The Momoir Project and The Yummy Mummy Club and many other parenting websites. Danielle lives with her husband and daughters in Langley, BC, Canada. She publishes a blog where she writes about her days being a motherless mother.

WEBSITE: www.justdworld.wordpress.com

Marilyn J. Curry lives in San Francisco where she works as a licensed clinical social worker with foster care children. She has been writing since she was a teenager, but "rewriting" for the past fifteen years. Her essay "On Not Being Photographed by Diane Arbus" was published in *New York Stories* magazine and was selected as a notable essay in the 2006 *Best American Essays* collection.

EMAIL: mjcurry50@gmail.com

Sara Etgen-Baker's writing career began with an unexpected whisper when a teacher said, "You've got writing talent." She ignored the whisper and instead chose a career in business and teaching. She occasionally resurrected her inner writer when preparing curriculum, employee manuals, and so on. Meanwhile, she realized her aptitude as both a proofreader and an editor and edited professional publications, proofread textbooks, and authored instructional ancillaries. After retirement Sara began her freelance writing career. With her husband's encouragement, she writes magazine articles, personal narratives, and short stories—as an ongoing contributor to *Tiny Lights* and with two memoirs recently published in *Yesteryears Magazette*.

EMAIL: sab_1529@yahoo.com
WEBSITE: www.lightsinthewindow.wordpress.com

Laura McHale Holland's award-winning memoir, *Reversible Skirt*, was published in early 2011 by Wordforest. Her short fiction, features, and essays have appeared in *Every Day Fiction*, the *Vintage Voices* 2009 and 2010 anthologies, *NorthBay biz* magazine, the *Noe Valley Voice*, and the original *San Francisco Examiner*. Laura also heads the editorial department of a trade publication covering the electronic payments industry.

WEBSITE: www.lauramchaleholland.com

Diane Hurles lives in Chicago and works in public relations and financial development for the national headquarters of the YMCA (YMCA of the USA). A former *Lifestyle* reporter and editor for several small daily newspapers in Indiana, where she lived for thirty years before moving to Chicago, Diane began studying creative nonfiction almost four years ago. She has written a series of stand-alone pieces about her childhood —including this one— that she would love to weave together into a memoir some day. Diane is married and has one grown son.

EMAIL: dianehurles@yahoo.com

Pat Jackson-Colando, a licensed speech-language pathologist and public speaker, has written articles for newspapers, magazines, and periodicals and grants for nonprofit organizations. Her short stories have been included in several anthologies. She has received numerous awards for community service and enjoys writing while her husband watches sports on television.

EMAIL: talklady@sbcglobal.net.

Deborah Jones-Norberto has been an actress, clown, magician's assistant, secretary, waitress, singer, pianist, organist, conductor, and most recently, a writer. Adopted as an infant by an IBM executive and his wife, she inherited the rich background of the Jones/Abercrombie family. Finding out years later she was the birth daughter of a sailor and his then upper class wife has provided a wealth of material for memoir. Debbie has been published in *Tiny Lights: A Journal of Personal Narrative*, in various music-related publications, and in newsletters. Debbie lives forty miles north of New York City with her husband and three children.

WEBSITE: www.debjones-norberto.com

Jeanne Jusaitis, MA, lives in Petaluma, California, where she writes for all ages. Her novel, *Journey to Anderswelt*, is written for middle-grade children. Jeanne draws from her memories of growing up in northern California, her many years of teaching and consulting, and traveling through Europe. She is a member of California Writers Club and the Society of Children's Book Writers and Illustrators. She published "The Legend of Tilly" in *Vintage Voices* (2010) and "Mystery Man" in *Tiny Lights Online Journal*. Her play, *Apples by Day*, will be produced by the Pegasus Children's Theater in summer 2011.

EMAIL: mizitis@comcast.net

Barbara Kitscher is wife to Bill and mother to Andre, Aaron and Allen. She lives on four wooded acres that once belonged to her parents, south of the town of Petoskey, Michigan. Like her mother before her, she is blessed with an extended family that includes four grandchildren. After many years in the field of education, she now has more time to pursue other dreams, which include reading, writing, hiking, biking and growing and preserving her own food.

EMAIL: bkitscher@gmail.com

Maria H. Klassen has had stories swirling around in her head all her life. She has used them throughout her teaching career, and in her retirement she is putting them down on paper. Her love of travel and sense for adventure has taken her to the village of Neuendorf in the Ukraine where her mother grew up, making her Sunday afternoons with her mother even more memorable. She lives in the small Ontario (Canada) town of Dunnville, when she isn't traveling to far away places and visiting her two children Kristin and Jason wherever they have ventured in the world.

EMAIL: mhk2@sympatico.ca

Nancy LaTurner's contribution, "Motherless Child," is adapted from her unpublished memoir, *Passing through Customs: A New Mexico Family's Adventures Abroad*, a lively depiction of family life in the Foreign Service. She and her husband raised their son and daughter in Iran, Cameroon, New Zealand, Somalia, Dominican Republic, Austria, and Bolivia. Nancy's essays have been published in the *Albuquerque Almanac* and the *SouthWest Sage*. Her short stories and essays have won awards in both the *SouthWest Writers* and the *Writer's Digest* annual contests. She writes from her home on Albuquerque's west side where coyotes and roadrunners roam.

EMAIL: nlaturner@yahoo.com

Ana Manwaring writes, edits, and teaches creative writing. She's branded cattle in Hollister, outrun gun totin' maniacs on lonely highways, lived on houseboats, consulted *brujos*, visited every California mission, worked for a private investigator, swum with dolphins, and writes about it all. Read her lifestyle column at www.petalumapost.com and follow her Mexico years at http://saintsandskeletons.blogspot.com. Ana is available for developmental editing and writing coaching. Coming soon, *Zihuatanejo*, a novel of intrigue in the Mexican resorts of Ixtapa and Zihuatanejo.

EMAIL: ana@anamanwaring.com
WEBSITE: www.anamanwaring.com

Rebecca Milford grew up among the sandstone buildings of Bath, UK, and now spends most of her time writing a novel in the little coffee shops that nestle in Clapham High Street, London. She also loves creating short stories and travel pieces and recently won the British Guild of Travel Writers award for new travel writing about an encounter she had in Japan. Ten years ago she had a kidney transplant, which is going well. She loves to read anything from the 1920's and hopes to one day make a living out of writing, now that she has completed a Masters in Creative Writing from Bath Spa University.

EMAIL: rebecca.milford86@gmail.com

Shelley Chase Muniz was born in Modesto, California, and attended college at Sonoma State University in Rohnert Park, California. She moved to Sonora in 1974, married, and had two children. She was a primary school teacher's aide and librarian at a local elementary school for fifteen years. She currently works at Columbia College as a library specialist. Shelley's short story, "Silent Screams," was a finalist in the 75th Annual Writer's Digest Short Story Contest. Last year another short story, "Holes," was published in the anthology *Wild Edges* by Manzanita Press. She has written a narrative nonfiction piece and a novel and is looking for publishers for both.

EMAIL: shelley.muniz@att.net

Katrina Norfleet makes her living as a marketing communications writer but feeds her soul writing fiction and creative nonfiction from her home in Maryland. Her work appears in the *Cup of Comfort for Christian Women* and *Victorious Living for Women* anthologies, *Our Voices* at www.BoomerWomenSpeak, various magazines, and her blog, Joy-Filled Life. She is a daughter and a mother of two, on the verge of becoming an empty nester.

WEBSITE: www.joy-filledlife.blogspot.com

Suni Paz, Argentine singer, songwriter, poet, educator, author, presenter, and recipient of numerous awards, has devoted her life to children and their families. She has thrilled worldwide audiences of all ages on stage, television, and radio with her stories and songs accompanied on guitar, charango, and percussive instruments. In 2007 Suni published her memoirs in Spanish, *Destellos y Sombras,* and in English, *Sparkles and Shadows.*

WEBSITE: www.sunipaz.com; LINKS: www.delsolbooks.com
SMITHSONIAN-FOLKWAYS: www.folkways.si.edu
RHAPSODY: www.rhapsody.com/suni-paz/bandera-mia-songs-of-argentina

Nekane Polo was born in Bilbao, Spain, in 1962. The oldest of four and the only girl, she first went to England for a month when she was eighteen and returned when she was twenty as an au pair. She then went to Paris in the same way where she met her Irish husband. She married in London in 1990 and did a few jobs as a freelance translator while having four children. The family moved to Ireland in 1998 and now she is trying to fulfill her dream as a writer.

EMAIL: nekanepd@yahoo.ie

Linda Sievers retired from Humboldt State University in northern California after twenty-six years of teaching dance. In 2006 she began writing memoir based on growing up in Illinois. She is married to watercolor artist and oil painter, Douglas Sievers. They have three daughters and three grandchildren. Linda recently moved to Cedar City, Utah, where she continues to write.

EMAIL: sieverslinda051@gmail.com

Clarice Stasz is Emerita Professor of History, Sonoma State University, whose scholarly books address issues of racism, sexism, and power in America. Her multigenerational biographies include *The Vanderbilt Women, The Rockefeller Women,* and *Jack London's Women.* In retirement she has returned to her youthful career aspiration, that of a musician and music teacher.

EMAIL: cstasz@comcast.net; WEBSITE: www.claricestasz.com

Mariana Swann was born in Bolivia and lived there for twenty years. She studied languages at the University of Geneva. She now lives in England and works as a foreign languages teacher while writing her Bolivian memoirs. As an adolescent, she witnessed social and political upheavals—she remembers the arrival of Che Guevara and the profound effect his ideals had on several members of her family. Mariana has just obtained a master's degree in Creative Writing from Goldsmiths College, University of London.

EMAIL: marianaswann@hotmail.com

Barbara Toboni writes short stories, poetry, memoir, and picture books. Her work has been published in literary journals, anthologies, and newspapers, including, *Cup of Comfort for Parents of Children with Autism, Tiny Lights Online Journal, Alura Poetry Quarterly*, and *The Napa Valley Register*. The author's most recent publication is a collection of poems, *Undertow*. She is a member of the California Writer's Club and the Society of Children's Book Writers and Illustrators. Born in Pennsylvania, the author lived in Guam for many years. She now writes in Napa, California, and dreams of moving day when she and her husband will retire in Plumas County.

WEBSITE: www.barbarasmirror.com

Angela Tung is a writer in San Francisco. Her work has appeared or is forthcoming in *Bellingham Review, CNN Living, The Frisky, New York Press*, and elsewhere. She is a regular contributor to *The Nervous Breakdown*, an online magazine featuring the work of published and emerging authors from around the world, and is a writer/editor at Wordnik.com, an online word source.

WEBSITE: www.angelatung.com

Elle Tyler (aka Ellen Whyte) has been involved in the arts her entire life. After many years of working in theatre, film, and TV, she married and became a full-time mom to an amazing son. During this time she trained and worked as a drama therapist using theater techniques that were developed to nurture the mentally ill. She facilitated workshops throughout the New York City area. After her mother's death, she began exploring photography and writing in an attempt to heal from her sadness. She now has a line of greeting cards and wall art that has been designed with the intention of promoting peace and tranquility.

EMAIL: premasun@aol.com

Elizabeth VanPatten lives in Napa, California. She enjoyed tennis, golf, hiking, birding and watercolor painting in her post-child-raising years until she discovered writing. In between sessions of scribbling, she pursued dryer lint art and had a show at the Winona Gallery in Mendocino featuring such characters as "Pork Tenderlint" and "Looselint the Shar-Pei" and other linty subjects— "Morning Tongue," "Dryer Degas," "Pestilints." She is currently in the process of self-publishing a children's book called *Nook and Granny and the Gazelle in the Gazebo*.

EMAIL: lizmuse@att.net

About the Authors: Introductions

Caryn Mirriam-Goldberg is the Poet Laureate of Kansas and the author of ten books, including collections of poetry, most recently, *Landed; The Sky Begins At Your Feet: A Memoir on Cancer, Community & Coming Home to the Body;* a beloved writing guide, *Write Where You Are;* and several anthologies. She is Founder of Transformative Language Arts—a master's program in social and personal transformation through the written, spoken, and sung word at Goddard College, Vermont, where she teaches. Mirriam-Goldberg also leads writing workshops widely. With singer Kelley Hunt, she co-writes songs, offers collaborative performances, and leads writing and singing Brave Voice retreats. She writes weekly columns and serves as poet-in-residence for www.TheMagazineOfYoga.com. Her daily blog posts, "Everyday Magic," include occasional podcasts and writing exercises.

BLOG: www.CarynMirriamGoldberg.wordpress.com
WEBSITES: www.BraveVoice.com; www.CarynMirriamGoldberg.com

Amber Lea Starfire is Publisher and Editor of *Writing Through Life*, a freelance editor, writer, and teacher. Her personal passion is to help others tell their stories and make meaning of their lives by accessing their inner wisdom and creative power through the act of writing. She has taught at community colleges and businesses for over twenty years and offers online courses and workshops in journaling, finding your voice, and the art of revising your writing. Amber is also the Coordinator for the Story Circle Network Online Classes Program and an active member of a Napa Writers Circle, the National Association of Independent Writers and Editors, and the International Association for Journal Writing. She is currently pursuing an MFA in creative writing while working on her memoir, A Mother Like Mine.

WEBSITES: www.writingthroughlife.com

Acknowledgements

I give sincere thanks to my writing club, the Redwood Writers, Sonoma County branch of the California Writers Club, who took me in—a transplant from the big city of San Francisco—and allowed me to help publish their annual anthologies. The support and friendship that came from my wine country tribe of writers created the foundation for this book.

Deep gratitude goes to those who first believed in the Wisdom project: Imara who saw the spirit need for mother-daughter legacy; Susan Bono, who brought her memoir expertise to burgeoning ideas; J. J. Wilson, who offered her famous "Sitting Room" as a cozy venue for the initial workshops. My special appreciation goes out to Lynn Henriksen who co-facilitated the Wisdom workshops, bringing her experience and encouragement to launch the work. I am grateful to web master and mentor, Linda Lee, who opened the website's window to the world and to Terry László-Gopadze for her generous modeling and courageous trailblazing with storytelling and women's truths.

In preparing the manuscript for publication, my thanks go to the editorial team: Ana Manwaring, Jeanne Miller, and Jane Merryman, who read and polished every word with care. For the book's layout and design, I acknowledge Jo-Anne Rosen for her patient skill and Cindy Pavlinac for her amazing work on the book cover with original images.

My heartfelt appreciation goes to each and every author for sharing her memoir about mother with craft, authenticity, forgiveness, and courage. These stories show the power of mother love, even when it is not evident, but missed. Each true memory has recognized the diverse but universal legacy of motherhood for our times.

I give thanks to my late mother, Terry Fischer, to my beloved grandmothers, great-grandmothers, and the long generations of women who have passed down the many ways of enduring love.

Finally, I am grateful to the publisher, Danny O. Snow, who saw value in promoting women's truths and women's voices years ago and continues to advance this work. I am also glad that his company, Unlimited Publishing, will seek new formats on the cutting edge of 21st century "content delivery systems" for this book and these stories.

— *Kate Farrell, Editor*

About the Editor

Kate Farrell, founder of the Wisdom Has a Voice project, earned her masters at the School of Library and Information Studies, UC Berkeley. She has been a language arts classroom teacher (pre-school and grades kindergarten through 12th), author, librarian, university lecturer, and storyteller in Northern California since 1966. She founded the Word Weaving Storytelling Project, based on her experience with storytelling and her belief in it, to encourage educators at all levels to learn and enjoy the art.

In 2006, when her mother passed away, Kate discovered in her mother's absence the deep influence her mother had always had on her life. Yet much of what was communicated had been unspoken—a tug of war of different priorities and directions. It wasn't until Kate let go with her mother's passing that she began to really understand her own mother. How much better to have accepted her mother's issues, history, and core truths earlier in life, while her mother was still with her.

Now Kate sees a new tradition of storytelling among women, that between daughter and mother. What was mother really trying to tell us? Sometimes she spoke in actions and not words. With this anthology Kate hopes to find out and share the wisdom of our mothers and the meaning daughters bring to this unique and deeply bonded relationship through memoir.

For more information about the ongoing Wisdom Has a Voice project, visit the website: www.wisdomhasavoice.com.

9410339R0013

Made in the USA
Charleston, SC
10 September 2011